OSTERLEY PARK

PARK

Middlesex

Eileen Harris

THE NATIONAL TRUST

Transport
LONDON UNDERGROUND: Osterley (Piccadilly line), $\frac{3}{4}$ mile;
STATION: Syon Lane, $1\frac{1}{2}$ miles; BUS: London Transport H91
Hounslow–Hammersmith, to within $\frac{1}{2}$ mile; CAR: via Thornbury
Road on the north side of the A4 betwen Gillette Corner and
Osterley Underground Station. Exit Junction 3, M4.

Acknowledgements
Lord Jersey has kindly contributed an introduction, commented on
the rest and helped in numerous other ways. I have also benefited
greatly from the advice and assistance of the following people, and
I should like to thank them: Alan Dodd, Richard Garnier, Mark
Girouard, John Harris, Richard Hewlings, Frank Kelsall, Susan
Palmer, Alison Turton, Philip Winterbottom, James Yorke, and the
staff at the Soane Museum and the Victoria & Albert Museum. The
entries on the ceramics have been written by Anthony du Boulay.

Eileen Harris

Photographs
Robin Briault pp. 14 (top left), 16, 17 (top left and bottom right), 18, 30;
Trustees of Christ's Hospital, Horsham pp. 13, 14 (bottom right); Country
Life Picture Library pp. 41, 45; English Life Publications Ltd, Derby p. 9;
Greater London Record Office p. 77; Guildhall Library, London pp. 8, 71;
Trustees of the National Gallery, London p. 15; National Portrait Gallery,
London pp. 4, 7, 25, 32; National Trust pp. 33, 53; National Trust
Photographic Library/Bill Batten pp. 22, 50, 51, 52, 56, 57, 61, 62, 63, 66, 67,
back cover; NTPL/Oliver Benn p. 37; NTPL/Vera Collingwood p. 73 (top
and bottom); NTPL/Rupert Truman pp. 11, 26 (bottom right), 27, 70, 76;
Trustees of Sir John Soane's Museum pp. 21, 23, 28, 29, 65, 68; Trustees of
the Victoria & Albert Museum, London front cover, pp. 1, 20, 26 (top), 38,
39, 42, 43, 46, 49, 54, 58, 59, 72, 75.

First published in Great Britain in 1994 by the National Trust

© 1994 The National Trust
Registered charity no. 205846
ISBN 0 7078 0179 6

Designed by James Shurmer

Phototypeset in Monotype Bembo Series 270
by Southern Positives and Negatives (SPAN), Lingfield, Surrey (9468)

Printed in Great Britain by Balding + Mansell
for National Trust Enterprises Ltd, 36 Queen Anne's Gate,
London SW1H 9AS

CONTENTS

George, 9th Earl of Jersey; photographed by Bassano in 1931. He gave Osterley to the National Trust in 1949

MEMORIES OF OSTERLEY
by the Earl of Jersey

OSTERLEY is a lovely place on a fine summer's day, but I, my brother and sisters never looked upon it as home. Home was Middleton, some twelve miles north of Oxford; a large house (it was 100 yards from the kitchen to the dining-room) in a large park – real country, which Osterley nowadays is not. My grandmother once described Osterley as a very nice summer villa, which I expect was how Robert Child, the creator of the Adam house, himself looked upon it. Upton, near Banbury in Oxfordshire, was his country estate.

My earliest memories of Osterley go back to when I was quite small, seeing my grandfather, well wrapped up in rugs, being wheeled about in a wickerwork bathchair. That must have been shortly before he died in May 1915. When the family moved to Osterley in the summer, most of the Middleton household went too, for the permanent staff at Osterley was only four or five. I remember the cuckoos continuously calling in the woods. One year I looked out of the school-room window straight into the wide open orange beak of a young cuckoo in a nest in the wisteria below. (Incidentally, our school-room was the Etruscan Dressing Room.) In those days – I must have been about six years old – I did not really like or appreciate Osterley. I have been told I complained, 'It's like living in a museum. One is never allowed to touch anything.'

Once I was at school, my memories of Osterley are few. My parents were there for the London season and then came August the twelfth, when they would go to Lowther Castle in Westmorland as guests of Lord and Lady Lonsdale for the grouse shooting. We children would go for the holiday to Baglan, the family estate at Briton Ferry and Neath near Swansea. From there we would take Dan O'Shea's Ferry over the River Neath (where the Neath Bridge stands today) to the seaside at Jersey Marine.

I was thirteen when my father died. Osterley was then kept in wraps and only opened for my sister's coming-out season several years later. Osterley had always been a perfect place for entertaining. My grandfather had been Governor of New South Wales in 1890–3, and on their return to England my grandparents gave huge garden parties and entertained all the political and literary lions of the day. I once asked my grandmother how long it took for a horse-drawn carriage to get down to Osterley from the West End of London – a distance of about ten miles. 'Half an hour or so' was the answer. In the 1930s I couldn't do it in much less time in my Rolls Bentley.

After I left Oxford, I went to work at Child's Bank, No. 1 Fleet Street, living at Osterley in the summer. It seemed no weekend passed without some friend asking, 'I have a guest staying from America who would love to see your pictures/ furniture/garden. Can we drop in on the way to the country?' As a result I found myself acting as curator or guide, and so in the end I decided to open Osterley to the public, starting at Easter 1939. Other than Montacute and Knole, I was, I think, the first stately home owner to do so. Then came the war. At the time I was working in Lombard Street at Glyn Mills, which had bought Child's after my father's death. My partners and I had previously agreed to move one of the bank's branches to Osterley for the duration.

When the war ended, it was obvious that trying to live in a house like Osterley would be quite impractical. I arranged therefore to give the house and grounds to the National Trust. I am happy to find when I visit Osterley now that it no longer has the 'museum' atmosphere of my youth, but rather that romantic, lived-in feeling which Robert Adam designed for the newly wedded Robert and Sarah Child in the 1760s.

CHAPTER ONE

SIR THOMAS GRESHAM AND THE TUDOR HOUSE

The house nowe of the ladie Greshams, a faire and stately building of bricke, erected by
Sir Thomas Gresham Knight, Citizen and Merchant Adventurer of London, and
finished about anno 1577. It standeth in a parke by him also impaled, well wooded, and
garnished with manie faire ponds, which affoorded not onely fish and fowle,
as swannes, and other water fowle; but also great use for milles, as paper milles, oyle milles,
and corne milles, all which are now decaied (a corne mille excepted). In the
same parke was a verie faire Heronrie, for the increase and preservation whereof, sundrie
allurements were devised and set up, fallen all to ruin.

John Norden, *Speculum Britanniae*, 1596

Sir Thomas Gresham's (?1519–79) 'faire and stately' brick house replaced what he referred to early in 1564 as his 'poor dowsse howse at Oystreley'. The latter was probably the farmhouse belonging to Osterley farm, which was included in the 600 acres, stretching from Osterley Lane to the outskirts of Heston village, that he was licensed to impark in 1565. Later that year he acquired another 146 acres extending his estate north-eastwards to the Norwood boundary.

The attractions of Osterley were numerous and as much concerned with commerce and profit as with the convenience and pleasure of being just ten miles from the centre of London, yet away from the bustle and safe from the plague. Heston, according to the topographer John Norden, was 'A most fertyle place for wheate . . . accompted the purest in manie Shires. And therefore Queen Elizabeth hath the most part of her provision from that place . . .' It had ample water for milling; it was well wooded and within close reach of gravel pits, brick fields and kilns.

Gresham, however, had no need for another country residence. He already had two houses in Norfolk, Westacre Priory and Intwood Hall, and two in Suffolk, Ringshall and Mayfield. In addition, he had a house in Antwerp where he spent much of his time as commercial agent and adviser to the

Crown, and was building a great town house for himself in Bishopsgate. It may, thus, have been with a view to the coming of age of his only son Richard in 1565 that he began amassing land around Osterley in the early 1560s and turning it to profit by establishing one of the first paper mills in England. According to his friend, the poet Thomas Churchyard, it was he:

That hath greate wealthe, and might such treasure
   spare
Who with some charge a paper-mill began;
And after, built a stately work most rare
The Royal Exchange.

Tragically, Gresham's son died in 1564 at the age of twenty, depriving him of an heir of his own blood and removing the urgency to build a new house at Osterley. His bereavement is thought to have caused him to divert some of the wealth he would have spent on securing the future of his family to the benefit of the public. In 1565 he undertook to finance the building of an exchange for London's merchants based on the one at Antwerp. The Royal Exchange, completed in 1568 and officially opened by Queen Elizabeth in January 1571, was an exceptional and important building with an open loggia surrounding a court. It was built in the Flemish style, largely of materials imported from Flanders, by a Flemish mason, Hans

Hendrik van Paesschen. Van Paesschen may have been involved in the equally remarkable courtyard house that Gresham had just finished at Bishopsgate, and was later employed by Gresham's close friend and the Queen's chief minister, Sir William Cecil, at Burghley in Cambridgeshire.

Queen Elizabeth visited Gresham at Osterley at least twice. Her stay in 1576, when the house was evidently habitable, seems to have been quite eventful. It was celebrated on the one hand by an entertainment of songs and sonnets – 'the Devises of Warre, and a play at Austerley; her being at Sir Thomas Gresham's' – composed by Thomas Churchyard, but marred on the other hand by two women 'maliciously, diabolically, and illegally' tearing up and burning the fence and palings round the park 'to the great disturbance and disquiet of the said Queen'. Elizabeth's own contribution to the occasion, as related by Thomas Fuller, was to find

Sir Thomas Gresham (?1519–79), the builder of the first house at Osterley; painted by an unknown Flemish artist, c.1565 (National Portrait Gallery)

fault with the large size of the forecourt, 'affirming that it would appear more handsome, if divided with a wall in the middle'. To her surprise and pleasure, Gresham had her fancy fulfilled overnight. While some of his courtiers expressed 'no Wonder he could so soon *change* a building who could build a Change; others (reflecting on some known differences in this Knight's family) affirmed that any house is easier divided than united'. These family differences probably refer to Lady Gresham's discontent with the will Sir Thomas made in 1575 leaving his house in Bishopsgate to Gresham College.

Moses Glover's 1635 survey of Isleworth (now at nearby Syon House) provides what is believed to be a fairly accurate, though imperfectly drawn and not very detailed picture of Osterley. It shows the fenced park extending from the River Brent on the east to Heston on the west, from the Norwood boundary on the north to Wyke on the south. In the eastern half of the park was a string of six rectangular ponds fed by tributaries of the Brent. These were presumably made by Gresham for his mills, heronry and fish. There was also a tall hunting lodge with a turreted roof.

The main approach was from the south, from Brentford past Wyke Green (enclosed by Gresham in 1567) to a walled enclosure roughly in the centre of the park. There were two entrances on the east side, a pedimented one leading into the first of the two courts in front of the house, and a simpler one leading into the stableyard. A comparison of Glover's survey with John Rocque's map of 1741, coupled with careful observation of the ground floor where some Tudor brickwork has been revealed, tells us quite a bit about Gresham's house, though many questions still remain unanswered.

Its plan was more or less as it is today, excluding the corner turrets: nearly square with a central courtyard surrounded by a passage or loggia, perhaps inspired by the loggias at Gresham House and the Royal Exchange, and, opening off that, a single range of rooms. In the internal angles of the courtyard were four tall turrets, almost certainly stair turrets, rising well above the roof for better viewing, and shown by Glover carrying banners. A joint in the vault of the central cellar under the

7

The Royal Exchange, which was built in London by Gresham between 1565 and 1568 (Guildhall Library)

present Hall (but not in the flanking cellars) suggests that there may originally have been a wide porch, possibly of two storeys, projecting from the middle of the west side of the courtyard.

The house, though said to be 'beseeming a prince', had only two storeys and an attic, with projecting end bays on the principal front which faced east on to a fountain court. Its entrance is not shown in the centre and was probably, as at Chastleton in Oxfordshire, in the side wall of one of the projections, most likely the northern one, assuming that the kitchen was originally in the south-east corner where it is today.

Glover's sketchy drawing seems to show a hipped roof, which would be a remarkably advanced feature for English domestic architecture of the

1570s, too advanced even for the builder of the Royal Exchange. It is quite possible that the roof and the four symmetrically arranged windows on the kitchen block (as opposed to the three on the opposite side) were alterations made in the interval of almost 60 years between the completion of the house in 1577 and Glover's drawing in 1635.

Gresham died in 1579, leaving Dame Agnes, his widow, well provided for. The 'clere valew' of all the estates left to her amounted to £2,388 10s 6½d per annum. From Osterley she received only £187 per annum, as opposed to £240 from Mayfield and £751 from the Royal Exchange; and her income must have been somewhat reduced by the decay into which she allowed its mills and heronries to fall.

On her death in 1596 Osterley passed to Sir William Reade, her son by a previous marriage. However, he evidently preferred to continue living on the opposite bank of the River Brent at Boston

Manor, a property bought by Gresham from the Earl of Leicester in 1572. Osterley was let to Sir Edward Coke, afterwards Lord Chief Justice, who seems to have remained there after Reade's death in 1626, until his own death in 1634. Sir William Reade's children all met unhappy ends. His first son, Sir Thomas, died without issue in 1595, his second son was convicted of manslaughter, and his daughter, Anne, was allegedly poisoned by her husband, Sir Michael Stanhope. So the property passed to his three Stanhope granddaughters: Jane, Viscountess FitzWalter, Elizabeth, Lady Berkeley, and Bridget, Countess of Desmond. Bridget, having been disowned by her father and 'brought up in a cottage', became a lady-in-waiting to Katherine Villiers, wife of the 1st Duke of Buckingham. Her marriage in 1630 to Buckingham's nephew, George Feilding, 2nd Earl of Desmond, was the first of the important Villiers Buckingham connections with Osterley.

With the agreement of her sisters and co-heirs, Bridget and her husband were allowed the use of Osterley during their lifetime. They lived there with their five sons and two daughters from 1634 to 1655. The estate was then sold to the Parliamentary general Sir William Waller, popularly known as 'William the Conqueror', who was no stranger to the place. His maternal grandmother, Lady Dacre, owned extensive lands in Norwood, Hayes, Northfield and Southall, some of which became part of the Osterley estate. In 1664 Waller sold 364 acres in the western part to Anthony Collins of the Middle Temple, whose grandson of the same name married the daughter of the first Sir Francis Child.

After Waller's death in April 1668, an inventory was made of his goods and chattels at Osterley by the same Francis Child, then an assistant to the goldsmith Robert Blanchard, and three others. The inventory lists 46 rooms (including two passages, 'inner' rooms and an 'Upper Gallery') on two floors, starting on the first floor where the painted gallery, great parlour, dining-room, 'green satin room' and bedchambers hung with tapestries and velvet would have been located. The hall, little hall, little parlour, the kitchen, ancillary service rooms and probably the chapel were on the ground floor. The second or attic floor, called the 'third story', contained an upper gallery and several bedrooms.

Sir William's study, the laundry, linen-room and rooms for the coachman, falconer and cook may have been in the stable block rather than the house.

It was Waller's wish that Osterley be sold for the benefit of his spendthrift son; and so it was in 1670 to Daniel Farington, about whom nothing is known. He kept it for only a few years and probably never lived there before he sold it in 1674 to Sir William Thompson.

In March 1683/4, following Thompson's death, it was bought by the versatile Nicholas Barbon, doctor of physic, financier, building speculator *par excellence*, entrepreneur, founder of fire insurance in England – in short, an opportunist who capitalised on the Fire of London. Roger North, who negotiated Barbon's rebuilding of the Middle Temple, left a colourful pen portrait of him. From his sectarian father, called Praise God Barbon (being christened 'Unless-Jesus-Christ-had-died-for-thee-thou-hadst-been-damned'), he gained:

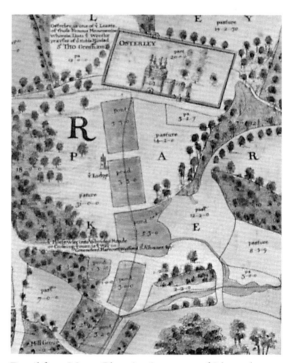

Detail from Moses Glover's 1635 survey of Isleworth (Syon House), which provides the only surviving view of Gresham's house

the knowledge of working the people ... with his much dealing in building, and consequently transacting with multitudes, he was an exquisite mob master ... He judged well of what he undertook, and had an inexpugnable pertinacity of pressing it through ... He never failed to satisfy everyone in treaty and discourse, and if he had performed as well he had been a truly great man. His fault was that he knowingly overtraded his stock ...

Barbon's principal purpose in buying Osterley was not profit, though admittedly the first thing he did was to use it as security to raise a very large sum of money. There was an element of self-aggrandizement in owning a large country estate within easy reach of London, but much more important was the association with Gresham, the renowned paragon of commercial acumen and success, whose Royal Exchange had inspired him to build Exeter Exchange in the Strand in 1676. Barbon's whole ambition was to live in the kind of 'mercantile magnificence' that Gresham did, and where better to do so than at Osterley.

Having paid £9,500 for Osterley, Barbon promptly raised a mortgage of £12,000 on it and Exeter Exchange, leaving him free to invest his capital more profitably. The money was put up by Roger Jackson (in trust for the Earl of Devonshire), Christopher Cratford (in trust for Francis Child), and Sir James Ward. According to evidence given by Child in a protracted Exchequer proceeding, Cratford and Jackson, having received no returns from their Osterley investment, brought an action of ejectment for recovery of the house in February 1689/90. A writ of *Facias Possessionem* was made in their favour, but before it was returned, Jackson found that 'Barbon had pulled down part of Osterley dwelling house and was making considerable alterations in the house which was not fit to be inhabited unless Barbon went on to finish'. It was agreed that 'Barbon should hold the house and garden, the warren house and tile-kilns as tenant-at-will of Jackson and Cratford and surrender the premises on demand', and that the rest of the estate should be let by Cratford and Jackson. But before the land was let, Barbon, an ace at 'contriving and shifting', had 'bought a Parliament-man's place, [and] had protection and ease'.

Although Jackson's findings were doubtless confirmed by the bank assistant sent to Osterley by Francis Child on 4 March 1690, definite visible evidence of what Barbon did is difficult to discover today. The horse stalls in the north range of the stable court can safely be credited to him. He was almost certainly responsible for pulling down the four stair turrets in the courtyard and replacing them with the two external turrets on the garden front, probably with the intention of building two more on the main front. The south-west turret still contains an open-well, timber newel staircase with turned balusters characteristic of the Barbon period, yet it is anachronistically called the 'Tudor stair'. While this was being built, the house might well have been 'unfit to inhabit', as Barbon claimed.

Some late seventeenth-century doors and mouldings can be seen in various rooms on the ground and chamber floors, but there is no certainty that they are in their original positions, for old woodwork and carving were constantly reused in the eighteenth-century renovations. The steward's room and the room adjacent to it on the ground floor of the south range would most likely have been wainscoted in Barbon's time. What we see today, however, is a convincing pastiche made in the late nineteenth or early twentieth century using some late seventeenth-century materials. A distinction may be drawn between the self-conscious historicism of this work and the continuity of the normal, economical practices of earlier periods.

Barbon ran out of money and died in debt in August 1698 before completing his renovation of Osterley. Precisely what his intentions were is unknown, but they were bound to have been grand and to have been determined by his admiration for Gresham, which may have made him one of the earliest revivers of the Tudor Gothic style. Whatever he planned was entirely for his own benefit, as he had no children and no interest in establishing a family seat. Though he may have lived in only part of the house, his way of life there was sure to have been up to his standards in London where, according to North, he 'lived as lord of the manor', in a 'capital messuage' in Crane Court, Fleet Street and was frequently to be seen 'as fine and as richly dressed, as a lord of the bedchamber on a birthday'.

In the 1690s Nicholas Barbon probably added the arched Tuscan doorway and the horse stalls behind it to Sir Thomas Gresham's stable block

CHAPTER TWO
THE CHILD FAMILY

The rise of the family of goldsmith bankers responsible for the transformation of Gresham's Osterley began in the second half of the seventeenth century with Francis Child. He was eighth of the eleven children of Robert Child, a prosperous clothier of Heddington near Devizes in Wiltshire where the Childs had been established since the sixteenth century.

Francis Child was born in December 1642 and sent at the age of fourteen to London to serve for eight years as apprentice to a goldsmith, William Hall. Having gained his freedom of the Goldsmiths' Company in 1664, he joined the firm of Robert Blanchard. Blanchard had recently married Margaret Wheeler, widow and heir of William Wheeler, an extremely successful goldsmith whose assistant he had been before the latter's death in 1660. This was a difficult time for Blanchard's firm, with the great plague of 1664–5 followed by the Fire of London in 1666, and Charles II's sudden closure of the Exchequer in 1672. But for Francis Child it was happy and rewarding, for through his work he met and on 2 October 1671 married Elizabeth Wheeler, Margaret Blanchard's only child and sole heir to the combined Wheeler and Blanchard fortunes.

By 1677 Blanchard and Child were partners, and the firm had extended its shop at Temple Bar into adjacent premises at 1 Fleet Street, known as the Marygold, the sign under which Child & Co. still operates. The marigold looking up to the sun with the motto *Ainsie mon âme* ('Thus my soul'), refers to the faithful bond between the flower and its god, the sun.

Over the years the business that Child inherited from Blanchard after his death in 1681 had come to function not so much as goldsmiths, making and selling gold and jewellery, but more and more as a bank, accepting valuables and money for safe keeping, giving receipts for deposits, which became assignable like cheques, and making loans against them. Child, in partnership first with his cousin, John Rogers, a former assistant of Blanchard, and later with a Mr Jackson (probably Roger Jackson, goldsmith) revived his jewellery business, which by the end of the century was one of the largest in London. In 1698 he was appointed Jeweller in Ordinary to William III.

Banking and goldsmithing and a certain amount of property speculation made Francis Child richer and richer. And as his wealth increased, so too did his participation and standing in City affairs. In 1689 he was elected an alderman and was knighted. He became Lord Mayor of London in 1698 and spent £4,000 on his inauguration, reviving the pageants that had not been seen for years. He represented Devizes in several parliaments and was one of four MPs for the City in the first parliament called by Queen Anne in 1702. He was President of Christ's Hospital, where he financed the rebuilding of the east ward in 1705. He was also a director of Greenwich Hospital and thus sat on committees with Sir Christopher Wren and John Evelyn.

Having advanced large sums of money to William III for the War of the Grand Alliance, he had an interest in the Treaty of Ryswick, near The Hague, which ended it, and was involved in the negotiations there in the summer of 1697. During his travels through the Low Countries, Flanders and Germany he purchased a large equestrian portrait of the 1st Duke of Buckingham and *The Glorification of the Duke*, both painted by Rubens (see p.15).

At this date Sir Francis's principal residence was Holly Bush House at Parsons Green, then the most fashionable district of Fulham. It was a stately brick mansion with a very good garden, which he inherited from Mrs Blanchard on her death in 1686, and subsequently enlarged and improved. There he

Sir Francis Child the Elder (1642–1713) in his robes as Lord Mayor of London (Christ's Hospital, Horsham)

Child's Banking House is immediately to the left of the Temple Bar in this mid-eighteenth-century view of Fleet Street by Thomas Bowles (private collection)

and finally Samuel, the youngest of the family. Sir Robert Child, who was knighted in 1714, succeeded his father not only as director of the bank, but also as MP for Devizes and President of Christ's Hospital. In addition he was a director of the East India Company in 1719–20. In 1703 he wrote offering to sell a painting by Lanfranco to the collector and amateur architect Thomas Coke of Melbourne, Derbyshire for what he paid for it (111 guineas) in gratitude for favours received from Coke's father-in-law, Philip Stanhope, 2nd Earl of Chesterfield. Payments in 1704, for a statue of Diana and vases for Lincoln's Inn Fields also suggest that he was something of a connoisseur. He is recorded as being in Padua in 1707, and his portrait painted in

Sir Francis Child the Younger (1684–1740), also painted as Lord Mayor (Christ's Hospital, Horsham)

and his wife lived with their eleven sons and three daughters.

Though Sir Francis could easily have afforded an even smarter, less suburban area, Parsons Green evidently suited his needs and he had no wish to move further from his business. On the contrary, what he most required was a substantial town house, larger than his freehold in Hemlock Court in the City. In 1702 he purchased 42 Lincoln's Inn Fields where he made extensive improvements before hanging his collection of 61 paintings, including the two Rubenses.

Meanwhile he was attempting to gain possession of Osterley, not as another place to live, but rather to protect the mortgage he had made to Nicholas Barbon, which was unpaid at the time of the latter's death in 1698. It was only a few months before Sir Francis's own death on 4 October 1713 that he finally obtained full possession of the estate.

Sir Francis was succeeded by his three surviving sons: Robert, the eldest, then Francis, his fourth son,

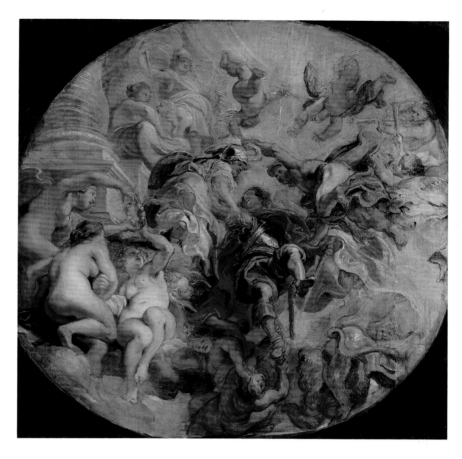

Rubens's sketch (in the National Gallery) for his 'Glorification of the Duke of Buckingham', which was bought by Francis Child the Elder in 1697. The finished painting once hung over the Grand Stairs at Osterley, but was later removed and has been replaced by a copy

1712 by Michael Dahl shows him in front of the Colosseum.

In 1720, the year after his mother's death, Sir Robert let the family house at Parsons Green to Admiral Sir Charles Wager, and was the first member of the family to live at Osterley. A veined marble chimney-piece made for the house in that year by Edward Stanton, master mason of Westminster Abbey, must have been part of a larger, albeit unrecorded scheme of improvements which he did not live to complete. He died unmarried in October 1721. Francis, on whom the mantle fell next, had considerably longer as head of the bank and owner of Osterley – nineteen years in all – until he died in 1740. In that period a great deal of work was done at Osterley (see Chapter Three).

The younger Francis was even more eminent than his father, and richer too. He was a director of the East India Company for seventeen years, and alderman of London, Prime Master of the Goldsmiths' Company in 1723–4, and President of Christ's Hospital, where he built a new courtroom. He was a Tory MP for the City from 1722 to 1727, and for Middlesex from 1727 until his death. His sympathies were with the Old Pretender from whom he received a friendly message on the occasion of his election as Lord Mayor in 1731. Despite his Jacobite leanings, he was knighted the following year.

The next in line should have been Francis's brother Stephen, then living at Richmond where he died in 1762. Perhaps because he had left Child's Bank and joined the goldsmithing firm of Mr Tudman at the Crown in Lombard Street, Stephen was passed over for the youngest brother, Samuel, who had been a partner for at least twenty years.

Of the fourteen children of Sir Francis the Elder, only Samuel and his three sisters married. Martha married a well-known deist, Anthony Collins, and had two daughters; Elizabeth married Tyrringham Backwell of Tyringham Hall in Buckinghamshire, son of Alderman Edward Backwell, the most important goldsmith banker in the reign of Charles II, and had six children including two sons, Barnaby and William, who were Samuel's partners in the bank; Jane married William Guyott and had no children. Samuel himself married Agatha, daughter of Mileson Edgar, in 1730 and had four sons and one daughter, who died young. When he inherited in 1740, he left his freehold house at Ham on the other side of the Thames and moved with his wife and four surviving sons – Samuel, James, Francis and Robert – to Osterley which he used as a country residence, keeping up his brother Francis's pack of hounds.

While Sir Francis the Younger held sway in the City, Samuel remained very much in the background and only after he inherited was he drawn into politics. In the parliamentary election of 1747 he was returned for Bishop's Castle, a notoriously corrupt Shropshire borough controlled by John Walcot, who was heavily in debt to Child's Bank. Samuel died in 1752 leaving Osterley and his shares in the bank in trust to his wife until his eldest surviving son, Francis, came of age in 1756.

After more than half a century a new generation was in charge, which was very different from the last. The third Francis Child was the first of the many owners of Osterley to have been brought up there and who could regard it as his family home. Unlike his forbears, he had not been trained as a goldsmith, but was educated with the nobility and gentry at Westminster School and Magdalen College, Oxford. Allan Ramsay's portrait of 1758 shows him to have been a handsome young man. He was cultivated, but unsophisticated when it came to building; socially ambitious and of course vastly rich. He came into his fortune early in 1756 and immediately used £2,000 of it to purchase the whole of the large and valuable library of the late Bryan Fairfax before it was dispersed at auction. The fact that Fairfax, a Commissioner of Customs and great friend of Lord Burlington, was also a cousin by marriage both of Francis and of George Villiers, 1st Duke of Buckingham was doubtless as important as the contents of his library. Having made this great acquisition, Francis promptly embarked on major improvements at Osterley (see Chapters Three and Four).

In January 1757, before Osterley was anywhere near finished, he spent £17,700 on buying Upton, a large classical house of 1695 in Warwickshire (now also a property of the National Trust), which gave him a proper country seat for hunting. Having spent £1,200 on his election in 1761, he was returned as Tory MP for Bishop's Castle. Marriage was next on the agenda and in 1763 he became engaged to Maria Constantina, daughter of Robert Trevor, heir to the large Buckinghamshire estate of the Hampden family, whose name he added to his own. Trevor Hampden was a member of Grenville's administration of 1763–5, a distinguished collector of prints and drawings and an amateur architect. Osterley was 'all prepared for a wedding

Francis Child (1735–63), who commissioned Robert Adam to rebuild Osterley in 1761; painted in 1758 by Allan Ramsay (private collection)

Robert Child (1739–83), who saw through Adam's transformation of Osterley; painted by Joshua Reynolds (destroyed by fire)

parliament for Wells in 1766 and held the seat until his death in 1782, but seldom attended. Nor was he active in the running of the bank, though he was its titular head and his share of its profits was estimated to be at least £30,000 per annum. There being no necessity for him to live near the bank, he sold the house in Lincoln's Inn Fields in 1767 and bought 38 Berkeley Square from the Duke of Manchester. Here the Childs spent the winter seasons from December to May in style, having employed Robert Adam to redecorate their several reception rooms and John Linnell to furnish them. For hunting and shooting the family went to Upton, where improvements were also made to the house and garden.

Osterley, however, was their principal residence, where they lived from June to November. Horace Walpole, a neighbour both in Berkeley Square and in Twickenham, called it their 'palace sans coronet', for Robert spared no expense to complete the remodelling of the house begun by Adam for his brother and to fill it with a profusion of porcelain,

'Rapid Westmorland' – John, 10th Earl of Westmorland (1759–1841) – eloped with Sarah Anne Child in 1782; painted by John Hoppner (private collection)

and posterity' when suddenly, on 22 September 1763, on the eve of the joyous event, Francis Child died. According to Horace Walpole, he left his beautiful bride-to-be a handsome legacy of £50,000, to which his brother added the diamonds that had been prepared for her.

This 'shocking accident' must have cast a shadow over the marriage a fortnight later, on 6 October, of Francis's 24-year-old brother and heir Robert to Sarah, daughter of Gilbert Jodrell of Ankerwycke House, Wraysbury, Buckinghamshire. Perhaps it, together with the death of his mother in January of that year, brought on the illness that caused Robert to withdraw as candidate for Aylesbury in the by-election in January 1764. He was returned to pictures and drawings, much of it collected by Sarah Child. She was a lady of considerable taste and above all a skilled needlewoman. Examples of her work can still be seen in the house.

A male heir to the century-old banking family and its immense fortune must have been very keenly hoped for. However, the Childs had only a daughter, Sarah Anne, born in August 1764. When she was seventeen and still a minor, this highly eligible and vivacious young lady fell in love with John Fane, 10th Earl of Westmorland, a neighbour in Berkeley Square. 'Rapid Westmorland' lived up to his nickname. Having discovered that Robert Child did not consider him a suitable son-in-law, he slyly asked one evening, 'Child, suppose that you were in love with a girl, and her father refused his consent to the union, what should *you* do?' 'Why run away with her, to be sure!' was Child's rash

Sarah, Lady Ducie (1741–93), the widow of Robert Child, with their daughter Sarah Anne, Countess of Westmorland (1769–93); by John Russell (private collection)

response. Westmorland needed no further encouragement, and early on 17 May 1782 the young lovers slipped out of Berkeley Square bound for Gretna Green. The Childs soon discovered what had happened and set out in hot pursuit, dispatching two servants on fast horses to apprehend the couple. As the horsemen were about to overtake them, the Earl drew his pistol, but was reluctant to fire, until Sarah Anne cried, 'Shoot, my Lord!' Emboldened by her words, he shot one of their pursuers' horses, and the Childs soon gave up the chase. The couple were married the next day in an ale-house in Gretna Green, but seem to have been forgiven fairly quickly. Robert Child gave his consent to a second, private marriage on 5 June at Apethorpe, Lord Westmorland's seat in Northamptonshire, but the dramatic upset was evidently too much for him and on 28 July he died, aged 43, it is said of a broken heart. His monument in Heston parish church was designed by Robert Adam.

His will attracted considerable attention when it was published, for it left the whole of his fortune not to his daughter, but to her second child, male or female, thereby preventing it from going to the main branch of the Westmorland family. The future heir was to 'take and use upon all occasions the surname of Child only'.

In accordance with his wishes, his widow maintained Osterley, Upton and Berkeley Square in the manner that he had kept them. Even after her marriage to Lord Ducie on 23 May 1791, she continued to live at Osterley and Berkeley Square. On her death in May 1793, which was followed in November by the death of her daughter Lady Westmorland, the bank and all Child's properties, including the manor and castle of Rochester, the manor of Swanscombe in Kent, properties in Lincolnshire, Warwickshire, Oxfordshire, Somerset and London, went to her granddaughter Lady Sarah Sophia Fane.

CHAPTER THREE
THE EARLY EIGHTEENTH-CENTURY HOUSE

Unlike Dr Nicholas Barbon, Sir Francis Child the Elder had no particular desire to own Osterley. He had become involved as a mortgagee strictly for profit, and acquired the estate by chance and by degrees, only gaining full possession in 1713 when he was 71 years old and had months to live. The great Elizabethan house had stood empty for fifteen years with Barbon's alterations left unfinished, and must have been in a lamentable state. Repairs and improvements were begun by his son, Sir Robert Child, and continued almost without stop by Sir Robert's brothers, Sir Francis the Younger and Samuel. They had no comprehensive plan and quite conservative taste.

One family of carpenters, the Hillyards, served them for over half a century – at the bank, at all their other properties in the City, at Parsons Green, Lincoln's Inn Fields, at Ham and at Osterley. Henry Hillyard, who started working for them in the 1690s, was followed by Benjamin in the 1720s and Matthew in the 1750s. These Hillyards may have been related to Thomas Hillyard, who supplied oak for St Paul's Cathedral, and the carpenter Francis Hillyard, who was one of the principal developers of Berkeley Square in the 1730s and '40s. In 1726 and 1727 Sir Francis Child the Younger paid Benjamin Hillyard a total of £2,471 17s for work at Osterley. Exactly what this major building operation consisted of and what other works there were – bricklaying, glazing, etc. – is not known.

The stables and offices were almost certainly altered around this time. By 1741, when Rocque drew his plan, some of the buildings shown in Glover's 1635 survey had been demolished, and the east range of the present stable court added, thereby shortening the original court that was still entered on the main front. The south and east ranges of this court were demolished later, probably in the 1750s or '60s.

What we see today is mainly an eighteenth-century evocation of the Tudor period based on the stables at Hampton Court. Some original features were incorporated and old bricks and stonework were reused to build the rest. William Kent's clock-tower at Hampton Court is another nearly contemporary example of the use of the Tudor Gothic style in association with a building of that period.

The north range contains Barbon's late seventeenth-century stables entered by a large, arched Tuscan doorway, probably of the same date. This entrance is slightly off-centre in relation to the court façade and not exactly aligned with the somewhat later clock-tower above, which is centred. The clock was made by Richard Streeter of Jermyn Street, clockmaker and Warden of the Clockmakers' Company, and is signed and dated 1714; the bell was made by Thomas Swaine in 1753. There are additional stables and a coach-house in the east wing, which was previously a barn. The grandiose stalls here date from the late 1730s or '40s and were modelled on a design by Inigo Jones for Holland House, which was published by Isaac Ware in 1731.

The west wing was evidently used as a brew-house, laundry and wash-house, with servants' accommodation on the first floor. A new dairy, bakehouse and privies were added on the garden side in 1764 and removed in 1950. Sophie de la Roche visited the dairy in 1786 and was enraptured by its splendid array of white milk-pails and butter-tubs with brass mounts 'gleaming like gold', and large Chinese butter dishes, tumblers and saucers, 'strewn all around on grey marble tables'.

Rocque's plan shows the west front of the early eighteenth-century house with towers at the angles, probably added by Barbon, and the east front with projecting wings aligned on the central avenue of a great formal garden created by Sir Robert or Sir Francis the Younger, or both. It was most likely

The clock-tower on the roof was added to the stables in the eighteenth century

Sir Francis who raised the height of the house in order to create a proper third storey in place of the dormer-windowed attic. This allowed the first floor to be treated as the *piano nobile* and the principal entrance to be moved up from the ground floor, which henceforth was used as a basement for services.

The entrance hall was placed in the centre of the east front and reached by a wide perron (flight of stairs), which was retained by Adam, though its top step had to be lowered in respect to the proportions of his Ionic portico. Above the hall was the library. We shall return to these rooms later.

There were pediments in the centre of the west

and south fronts and presumably on the east and north fronts as well. When these were added is not known; only those on the east and west fronts were retained. The red-brick walls of the house would not have been quite so prominent in the early eighteenth century as they are now, for, apart from the pediments to relieve the eye, the top-floor windows were taller and there was a stone string course beneath them.

Samuel Child, who owned the house from 1740 to 1752, removed the projecting wings on the east front and replaced them with angle turrets like those on the garden front. Their stone quoins, being only on the upper floors, reinforce the perception of the ground floor as a basement, and must therefore post-date the building of the perron.

The next important phase of remodelling began

in 1756, when the new incumbent, Francis Child, came of age. His first priority was to accommodate the large collection of books belonging to the late Bryan Fairfax, which he had just bought *en masse*. The library, a sizeable room of 1,167 square feet located in the centre of the east front above the hall, was promptly fitted with bookcases framed by Ionic pilasters, part old, possibly from the Barbon period, and part new. When this section of the house was demolished to make way for the open portico, the collection of books, which was prized as one of the principal treasures of Osterley, was relocated in the new Library designed by Adam. Some of the cases from the earlier room were re-erected in a passage behind the Library.

The late 1750s saw Venetian windows inserted at both ends of the Gallery, which ran the length of the west front; the chamber windows shortened; quite a bit of reroofing; water-closets installed in some of the turrets; old doors and shutters, cornices and architraves, mouldings and panels adjusted and new ones made. By 1759 Francis Child's bedroom and the billiard-room were finished and hung with pictures. The 'first chamber', later called the Yellow Taffeta Bedchamber, was ready and so too was the Gallery, except for its chimney-pieces.

The man responsible for all this work was Matthew Hillyard, who, like many experienced carpenters of the period, did not require the intervention of an architect. Boulton Mainwaring, a practising surveyor trained as a joiner, seems to have acted as clerk of the works and intermediary between Child and his employees, ordering work from specialist craftsmen as well as examining and paying their accounts. He was still serving Robert Child in this capacity in 1777, and may be identified with 'Mr Mainwaring, the Steward', who was living in a house in Norwood on the Osterley estate in 1774.

It would have been Mainwaring's job to contract

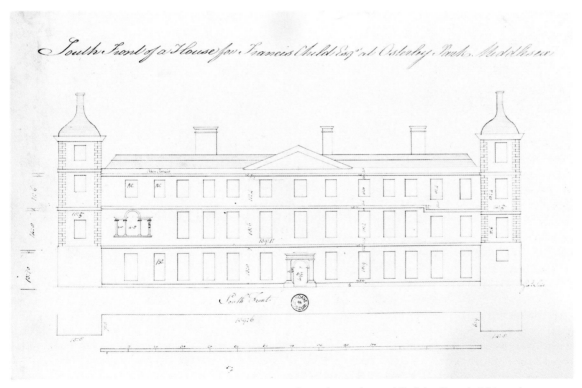

An anonymous survey of the south front, made about 1760, before Adam took over (Sir John Soane's Museum)

Detail of the Gallery chimney-piece, carved by Joseph Wilton from a design by William Chambers and put up in 1764

with a sculptor to supply the marble chimney-pieces required for the old hall and the Gallery. The commission went to Joseph Wilton, who procured designs from the architect William Chambers, a close friend with whom he had been in Rome. This would explain the presence of Wilton's signature on Chambers's design for chimney-pieces for the hall, which came into Adam's possession and is amongst his drawings at the Soane Museum. Wilton was directly involved with Osterley, but Chambers was not. Whether the hall chimney-pieces were executed to Chambers's design is not known. If they were, they would have been removed when Adam opened the centre of the east front.

The marble chimney-pieces in the Gallery were adapted from a design by Chambers (now in the

Chimney Pieces for the Hall at Osterley / of Roach Abbey Stone.

Jos.ᵗ Wilton. Sculp.ᵗ

Joseph Wilton's design for a chimney-piece in the pre-Adam entrance hall (Sir John Soane's Museum). If ever executed, it was swept away when Adam opened up the east front

Avery Library, New York) and installed by the bricklayer Richard Norris in 1764, by which time Adam was in full command. Though designs by Chambers for the chimney-pieces in the Yellow Taffeta Bedchamber and Mr Child's Bedroom may also have been obtained through Wilton, he did not execute them. They were the work of a specialist woodcarver, possibly William Linnell or his son John, who supplied the chimney-piece in Mrs Child's Dressing Room.

There is no conclusive evidence of any other work at Osterley by Chambers; nor was Francis Child a subscriber to his *Treatise on the Civil Part of Architecture*, published in the spring of 1759. The mishmash of remodelling done in the first half of the eighteenth century reveals the hand of an artisan architect like Mainwaring, Hillyard or Norris, but certainly no one of the calibre of William Chambers. Nowhere is the absence of professional architectural direction more apparent than in the survey of the south front of the house as it was in about 1760, with a Venetian window at the west end, a broken string course at the east end, a large floating pediment in the centre and two Tudor Gothic turrets with ogee cupolas framing the whole.

To bring the botched Elizabethan pile into line with fashionable Neo-classical taste was the challenge that awaited Robert Adam.

CHAPTER FOUR

ROBERT ADAM AT OSTERLEY

Robert Adam's intervention at Osterley in 1761 brought to an end the long period of piecemeal repairs and incoherent additions made by the carpenters, bricklayers and other craftsmen habitually employed by the Childs in all their London properties. In its place he provided the comprehensive direction that transformed the dowdy old house into what Walpole extolled as 'the palace of palaces ... so improved and enriched, that all the Percies and Seymours of Sion must die of envy'.

The command of classical antiquity that Adam had gained in Italy between 1754 and 1758, boosted by his brash self-confidence and flamboyance, quickly marked him as the new leader of London fashion and made him a buzz on the London scene. At Hatchlands in Surrey (1758–61), Shardeloes in Buckinghamshire (1759–63), Harewood House in Yorkshire (1759–71), Croome Court in Worcestershire (1760), Kedleston in Derbyshire (1760–70), Syon in Middlesex (1760–7), and Compton Verney in Warwickshire (1761) he took over from more conventional architects, among them James Paine and John Carr of York, Stiff Leadbetter and 'Capability' Brown. He offered something new and full of vitality, 'directed but not cramped by antiquity'. In his own estimation he had 'brought about a kind of revolution in the whole System of [the] useful, and elegant art of interior decoration'.

At Osterley we are fortunate in being able to see not only the contrast of the old and new styles, but also the several stages in the development of Adam's style from its early robustness and uncertainty to its mature fluency and characteristic delicacy.

Who recommended Adam to the young Francis Child is not known; however, there are at least two contenders. The 1st Duke of Northumberland, for whom he was working nearby at Syon, is one, but the most likely is Sir Francis Dashwood, later Lord Le Despenser, who got him the job of rebuilding the Shambles at High Wycombe in Buckinghamshire in 1761 and also commissioned designs for his own houses at Hanover Square and West Wycombe Park in this period. The Dashwoods, like the Childs, were a prominent family of aldermen and Lord Mayors in the City of London. Even more to the point was the fact that Dashwood supervised the affairs of his brother-in-law and nephew, John and Charles Walcot, whose debt to Child's Bank was well over £16,500. In consideration of this the Walcots arranged Francis Child's uncontested return as MP for Bishop's Castle in March 1761.

Adam was called upon by Francis Child not only to provide a master plan for giving the house a modern image, but also to reduce its size. This was a remarkable request so soon after the completion of the large library on the east front and the Gallery on the west. His proposal, set out in a section, plans and elevations dated 1761 at the Soane Museum, was to demolish the entire east front and reduce the north and south sides to the same length as the west side, thus transforming the courtyard house into a U-shaped one.

The Venetian windows inserted two years earlier were to be removed, and the house regularly fenestrated with tall windows on the *piano nobile* and square ones on the top floor, all in moulded surrounds. The ground floor was to be treated as a basement, with small windows and rusticated walls. The rest of the exterior was to be rendered in stucco. The Tudor porch projecting from the middle of the west side of the courtyard was to be brought forward and extended on each side to form the new entrance front, identified by a Corinthian portico reached by a short flight of stairs. Behind the hall, in the space intended for the gallery, was the library flanked by two small rooms. The new gallery was to be in a two-storey room occupying the whole of the south wing.

Robert Adam, the creator of Osterley; attributed to George Willison, c.1770–5 (National Portrait Gallery)

Section through Osterly House from West to East

Adam's first proposal for Osterley, showing a library (left) behind the entrance hall on the principal floor (Victoria & Albert Museum)

This solution evidently proved too drastic for Francis Child and was rejected, though some elements were eventually executed, notably the removal of the Venetian windows and floating pediments on the north and south sides, and the enlargement of the Tudor porch. The curved stairs on the garden front, shown on Adam's 1761 section, but not on his plan, may be an Adam addition, though presumably stairs of some description were planned for that position before his time, when the pediment was added. Adam was certainly responsible for the Etruscan-style grotto room under the perron and most likely for the large pedimented doorcase with an enriched Doric order opening into the Gallery.

Precisely what was decided or done over the two years before Francis's death in September 1763 is not known. There are no surviving accounts specifically for work at Osterley in this period, and only one design by Adam for the Doric Orangery. Adam's design for the east front with its unusual transparent portico is inscribed for Robert Child and was probably made early in 1764. This felicitous

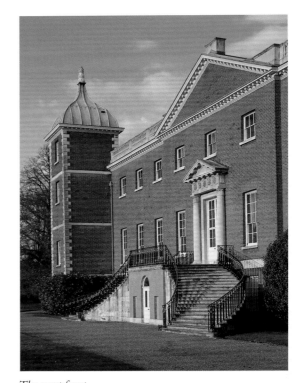

The west front

The 'transparent' portico on the east front

Neo-classical scheme has two possible classical sources, the Portico of Septimius Severus at Rome and Felibien's engraved reconstruction of Pliny's Tuscan villa. However, it was more immediately inspired by the early eighteenth-century portico proposed for the fourth side of the court of Witham Park, Somerset, which would have come to Adam's attention around 1762 when he was called upon by William Beckford to make designs for a new house.

The centre of the east front must have been demolished by May 1764, when the bricklayer Richard Norris blocked the doors to the former hall and library and made the 'footing to the New Front' on the west side of the courtyard. The stairs that had been built up to the *piano nobile* in the 1740s were retained, and the courtyard raised to the same level so as to enable direct entry into the new first-floor Hall. In order to compensate for the consequent loss of light in the ground-floor passages, a shallow open area was created around the raised courtyard, windows were inserted at the very top of the passage walls, and the floor level was raised.

Osterley was visited in 1772 by Agneta, widow of the Rt Hon. Charles Yorke, son of the 1st Earl of Hardwicke and Attorney-General. Agneta sent a fairly full description of the house to her sister, Letitia Beauchamp-Proctor. At that time the portico was 'not quite finished but there [were] already several very fine rooms'. A year later Walpole saw the house and wrote ecstatically to Lady Ossory:

There is a double portico that fills the space between the towers of the front, and is as noble as the Propyleum of Athens. There is a hall, library, break-fast-room, eating-room, all *chef d'oeuvres* of Adam, a gallery 130 feet long, and a drawing-room worthy of Eve before the Fall . . .

Adam's interiors at Osterley do not form a continuous sequence of stylistically homogeneous decoration. The Drawing Room and Eating Room were done first and probably in two or more stages, starting as usual with the ceilings, which may have

Design of a Ceiling for the Front Drawing Room at Robert Child Esq.ʳ House in Berkley Square.

Rob.ᵗ Adam Architect 1769

Adam's design for the drawing-room ceiling of Robert Child's Berkeley Square house (Soane Museum)

been decided upon before Francis Child's death. Their decoration is not as refined or as well integrated as other rooms of the period by him, for example those at Syon or Croome Court. Evidently the principal staircase was also decorated in two stages. The Library, by contrast, is all of a piece and dated 1766. Designs for the Hall were delayed until 1767 and 1768, probably owing to the building works connected with the raising of the courtyard and the formation of the new entrance front.

Between 1769 and 1771 work on Osterley was postponed while Adam's attention was focused on the decoration of Child's London house, 38 Berkeley Square. By then Robert Child had become an 'improving' addict, going from strength to strength inside Osterley as well as in the garden.

Regardless of the fact that state apartments were outdated by 1772, Child commissioned Adam to create one to follow on from his Palmyra-inspired Drawing Room, consisting of a Gobelins Tapestry Room, a velvet State Bedroom and a painted Etruscan Dressing Room. Unlike his earlier interiors at Osterley, these three rooms were conceived together as a sequence of different styles (French, English and Italian) and different colours (red, green and blue) alluding to the elements fire, earth and air. In Walpole's opinion the different materials 'Tapestry, carpets, glass, velvet, satin [were] all attributes of Winter', which he thought incongruous, tasteless and inappropriate. Notwithstanding, the State Apartment at Osterley is the only surviving example of the high watermark of Adam's interior decoration complete with the furniture he designed for it.

28

Adam's 1776 design for the needlework panel in the Etruscan Dressing Room, which was embroidered by Mrs Child (Sir John Soane's Museum)

CHAPTER FIVE

THE NINETEENTH AND TWENTIETH CENTURIES

Robert Child's granddaughter, Lady Sarah Sophia Fane, was only eight when she inherited Osterley and the Child fortune in 1793. By the time she came of age in 1806, she was the Countess of Jersey, wife of George Villiers (later Child-Villiers), 5th Earl of Jersey. Before Villiers succeeded to the title in August 1805, the newly-weds evidently expected to live at Osterley, and in February of that year spent the large sum of £762 on furniture and upholstery from the prominent firm of Marsh & Tatham. Probably there were other renovations, as the house had not been lived in since the death of Lady Jersey's mother twelve years before.

As it happened, the couple were not to make their home at Osterley, but rather at the Jersey family seat, Middleton Park in Oxfordshire. Over the next five years they made extensive additions and alterations there and also refurbished the Childs' house in Berkeley Square, which now became the Jerseys' London residence. Thomas Cundy was their architect.

Middleton was the heart of the celebrated equestrian activities of the 5th Earl: a breeder and owner of racehorses, including three famous Derby winners, Middleton in 1825, Mameluke in 1827, and Bay Middleton in 1836, twice Master of the Horse to Queen Victoria, and an ardent fox-hunter, whom 'Nimrod' described as 'one of the hardest, boldest, most judicious [and] perhaps the most elegant rider to hounds the world ever saw'.

While the elegant Earl was a pillar of the Turf, his Countess, commonly known as 'Queen Sarah', held sway in London society and was one of the six lady patronesses of Almack's Club, which was almost as exclusive as the Court. Perhaps because her mother-in-law had been the Prince Regent's mistress, she

(Left) 'Queen Sarah', Sarah Sophia, Countess of Jersey (1785–1867); by James Holmes (private collection)

was an active supporter of his estranged wife, Queen Caroline. Flattered for her wealth and admired for her beauty and conversation, despite her pushy, pretentious manner, she was called by Byron, 'The veriest tyrant that ever favoured fashion's fools.' There are swagger portraits of her by Lawrence and Romney; she also inspired Zenobia in Disraeli's novel *Endymion* and Lady St Julians in his *Coningsby*.

The Earl's expensive building works at Middleton, estimated to have cost £200,000, must have awakened him to the fact that even with his wife's fortune, he could not maintain their other houses – Baglan (a Jersey property at Briton Ferry in Neath), Upton and Osterley – in the style which they had established at Middleton and Berkeley Square. Upton and Baglan could be used for hunting, but Osterley was a conspicuous extravagance, especially in the climate of economic uncertainty that accompanied the Napoleonic wars.

In 1812 he received a report from his surveyor pointing out that the yearly expenditure of over £3,300 on the Osterley estate alone was 'certainly an enormous sum for the mere purpose of keeping up a house', and suggesting that either he find a suitable tenant – a 'nobleman, or high official character or a merchant of eminence' – who was 'sufficiently affluent to occupy so Magnificent a residence', or, as that was unlikely, that he 'pull down the house, dismantle the park and let out the estate upon building leases'. Fortunately he did nothing. The problem, as his racing friend Charles Greville saw it in 1829, was more complex:

Osterley is a very fine house, which is thrown away, as they hardly ever live there ... Middleton is the worst place in England, and now they regret it, but Jersey hates Osterley and likes Middleton.

In 1832 the house and grounds were put on the market for letting, but no suitable tenant was found

Margaret, Countess of Jersey (1849–1945) dressed as Anne of Austria for the Devonshire House Ball, 1897 (National Portrait Gallery)

and the despairing Earl was evidently driven to explore the possibility of building some villas in the park. Designs made by the architect John Davis Paine were exhibited at the Royal Academy to publicise the venture. That was in 1841, the year that Jersey's eldest son and heir, George Augustus Frederick, married Sir Robert Peel's daughter, Julia. George died aged 51 in 1859, just three weeks after he succeeded his father as 6th Earl. His heir, Victor Albert George, was aged fourteen.

Now there were plans to let Berkeley Square too, and an inventory was taken of the Dowager Countess's decorative furniture, valuables, china, bijouterie and objects of virtu in the principal reception rooms there. However, nothing happened and Lady Jersey went on receiving at Berkeley Square every evening. Her sister-in-law, Lady Westmorland, described her in old age:

She is still brilliant, talkative, gay, and beautiful; always dressed in the latest fashion, in sky blue or rose

colour, with flowers on her (own) hair, which is not grey . . . she has kept her sight, hearing and memory.

Her death in 1867 was followed in 1871 by that of her eldest surviving child, Frederick William.

At this stage attention was focused on Osterley, for a tenant was at last found in the person of Grace Caroline, Dowager Duchess of Cleveland, daughter of the 9th Earl of Westmorland and thus a first cousin of the late Sarah Sophia. In 1871 £3,200 was spent on painting, cleaning and repairs at Osterley to make it ready for her occupation. She presided over the house, 'stumping about with her ebony stick', until her death in 1883. Margaret Elizabeth Leigh (daughter of Lord Leigh of Stoneleigh), who married the 7th Earl of Jersey in 1872, described her as 'a fine old lady and an excellent tenant, caring for the house as if it had been her own'. According to Augustus Hare, she cared for the house 'far more than its owner Lord Jersey, and [did] much to beautify and keep it up'. What she did is not recorded.

After she died, the Jerseys' first idea was to relet the place, but before doing so they gave a garden party in 1884, which was so successful that they decided to keep it on as a suburban home. One garden party led to another and soon the Jerseys' Saturday to Monday parties at Osterley were famous. They were attended by politicians, princes, writers and other public figures, who were graciously received by Lady Jersey under the portico, and entertained in the Hall and the pleasure gardens. Henry James made Osterley the background of his novella, *The Lesson of the Master*, and Lionel Ashley characterized it in humorous verse written in the Osterley visitors' book in 1887:

In a cot may be found I have heard the remark
  More delight than in Castles with pillars.
But we find in the Palace of Osterley Park
  All the charms of suburban Villiers.

A Sunday in Osterley Gardens and Halls,
  That's a day to look on to and after.
Its pleasure my memory fondly recalls
  And the talk, with its wisdom and laughter.

(Right) The Drawing Room in 1898

However well Osterley had been cared for by the old Duchess, it was evidently in need of considerable repair and renovation. Something had to be sacrificed to make this possible, and reluctantly the Jerseys decided to sell the famous library with its ten Caxtons. The eight-day sale in 1885 raised over £13,000. Though the full extent and particulars of the work done in this period are not recorded, we can be sure that Lady Jersey, having made the house a hub of social activity, would also have done her best to make it presentable and comfortable for her numerous guests.

She was probably responsible for changing the colour of the Entrance Hall from light grey to Wedgwood blue and renaming it the Wedgwood Hall; for replacing the original green velvet hangings in the State Bedchamber with silk; and for painting the Library in shades of green following one of Adam's designs in the house. The yellow Breakfast Room was used as the family living-room and probably had major repairs, particularly to the ceiling and chimney-piece. Other anomalies in the house may also be credited to Lady Jersey. She treated Osterley like a home, using the Etruscan Dressing Room as a school-room for her children and sleeping in the State Bed herself when the rest of the bedrooms were full. On the whole, however, the Adam rooms were cherished as a 'museum'.

The 7th Earl died in 1915, having spent several years as an invalid being pushed around Osterley in a bath-chair while hospitality continued as before. He was succeeded by his son, George Henry Robert, who died in 1923 after only eight years as 8th Earl, during which time Osterley was used only on occasional summer weekends. The 9th and present Earl, George Francis Child-Villiers, was aged thirteen when he succeeded.

In June 1925 Lady Jersey, widow of the 8th Earl, remarried and the trustees decided to put in electric light and central heating in order to enable the house to be let. Concerned to protect the integrity of the Adam rooms, Lady Slessor, as she then was, brought in the Adam expert and curator of the Soane Museum, A. T. Bolton, who was also a practising architect, to direct the work. One of Bolton's most important contributions was the preservation of the vaulted servants' hall on the ground floor, which he suggested could be used as 'the future entrance hall' instead of being given over to heating installations.

The house, equipped with modern conveniences and a 'museum collection of old pictures, furniture, tapestries and *objets d'art*', was advertised for letting in *Country Life* in June 1926. Again, no suitable tenant could be found. At first the Jerseys used the house only for parties and occasional weekends; then in 1937–8 they lived there for eighteen months with a staff of twelve or more while Middleton was being demolished and a new house by Lutyens erected in its place, which has been called 'possibly the last great country house to be built in England'. The 9th Earl made some improvements to Osterley, including the provision of modern bathrooms, but was primarily interested in the garden (see Chapter Seven). Though he had no intention of living there permanently, he was insistent that the house and its contents be preserved intact and unaltered. Talk of Middlesex County Council buying it came to nothing and discussions with the National Trust faltered because there was no endowment. Lord Jersey himself opened it to the public for the first time at Easter 1939. Finally in 1949 he gave the house and the grounds to the National Trust. They were subsequently leased to the Ministry of Works, now the Department of the Environment, which maintained the property until 1991, when the National Trust took over the running of Osterley. The furniture was purchased by the nation and placed in the care of the Victoria & Albert Museum, which administered the house until 1991.

OWNERS OF OSTERLEY

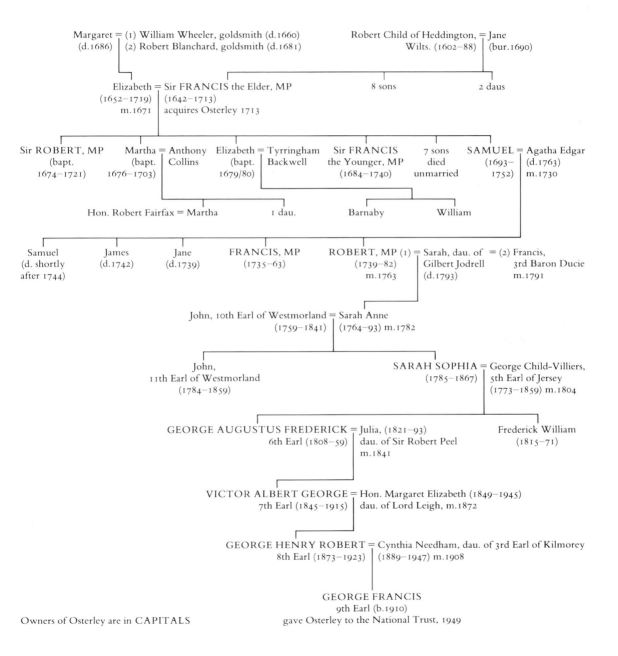

Margaret = (1) William Wheeler, goldsmith (d.1660)
(d.1686) | (2) Robert Blanchard, goldsmith (d.1681)

Robert Child of Heddington, = Jane
Wilts. (1602–88) | (bur.1690)

Elizabeth = Sir FRANCIS the Elder, MP
(1652–1719) | (1642–1713)
m.1671 | acquires Osterley 1713

8 sons

2 daus

Sir ROBERT, MP
(bapt.
1674–1721)

Martha = Anthony
(bapt. | Collins
1676–1703)

Elizabeth = Tyrringham
(bapt. | Backwell
1679/80)

Sir FRANCIS
the Younger, MP
(1684–1740)

7 sons
died
unmarried

SAMUEL = Agatha Edgar
(1693– | (d.1763)
1752) | m.1730

Hon. Robert Fairfax = Martha

1 dau.

Barnaby

William

Samuel
(d. shortly
after 1744)

James
(d.1742)

Jane
(d.1739)

FRANCIS, MP
(1735–63)

ROBERT, MP (1) = Sarah, dau. of = (2) Francis,
(1739–82) | Gilbert Jodrell | 3rd Baron Ducie
m.1763 | (d.1793) | m.1791

John, 10th Earl of Westmorland = Sarah Anne
(1759–1841) | (1764–93) m.1782

John,
11th Earl of Westmorland
(1784–1859)

SARAH SOPHIA = George Child-Villiers,
(1785–1867) | 5th Earl of Jersey
| (1773–1859) m.1804

GEORGE AUGUSTUS FREDERICK = Julia, (1821–93)
6th Earl (1808–59) | dau. of Sir Robert Peel
| m.1841

Frederick William
(1815–71)

VICTOR ALBERT GEORGE = Hon. Margaret Elizabeth (1849–1945)
7th Earl (1845–1915) | dau. of Lord Leigh, m.1872

GEORGE HENRY ROBERT = Cynthia Needham, dau. of 3rd Earl of Kilmorey
8th Earl (1873–1923) | (1889–1947) m.1908

GEORGE FRANCIS
9th Earl (b.1910)
gave Osterley to the National Trust, 1949

Owners of Osterley are in CAPITALS

35

PLANS OF THE HOUSE

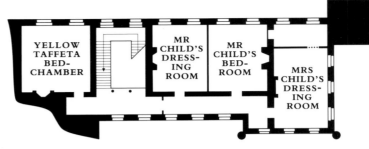

BEDROOM FLOOR

- YELLOW TAFFETA BED-CHAMBER
- MR CHILD'S DRESSING ROOM
- MR CHILD'S BED-ROOM
- MRS CHILD'S DRESSING ROOM

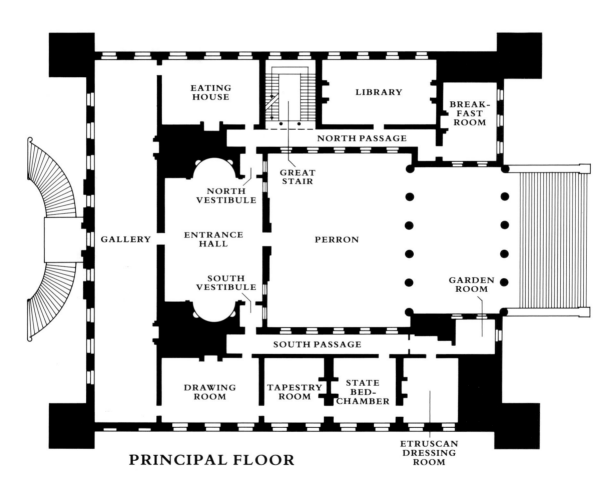

- EATING HOUSE
- LIBRARY
- BREAK-FAST ROOM
- NORTH PASSAGE
- GREAT STAIR
- NORTH VESTIBULE
- GALLERY
- ENTRANCE HALL
- PERRON
- GARDEN ROOM
- SOUTH VESTIBULE
- SOUTH PASSAGE
- DRAWING ROOM
- TAPESTRY ROOM
- STATE BED-CHAMBER
- ETRUSCAN DRESSING ROOM

PRINCIPAL FLOOR

N

(Right) The Hall

CHAPTER SIX

TOUR OF THE HOUSE

For the sake of clarity, the entrance front is assumed to face east, although in fact it faces north-east.

THE HALL

The Hall, entered directly from the raised courtyard, was designed by Adam in 1767 to replace the earlier hall that was demolished when the portico was created. It is rectangular in plan with large semicircular alcoves at the ends, each containing a fireplace flanked by niches filled with statues. These alcoves were intended not only to provide the diversity of shapes and play of light and shadow, the

'movement' upon which Adam set great store, but also to decrease the length of the room and thereby to increase its relative height, which contemporary visitors agreed was too low. To enhance further the appearance of height, Adam reduced the normal entablature to a shallow Greek-key frieze and elongated the pilasters, which are modelled on those he found in the ruins of Diocletian's palace at Spalatro (now Split in former Yugoslavia), the subject of his first publication in 1764.

Evidently the Hall was used as a saloon, reception-room and occasional dining-room, which is not surprising, as the house was normally entered on the ground floor through a 'rustick door' on the

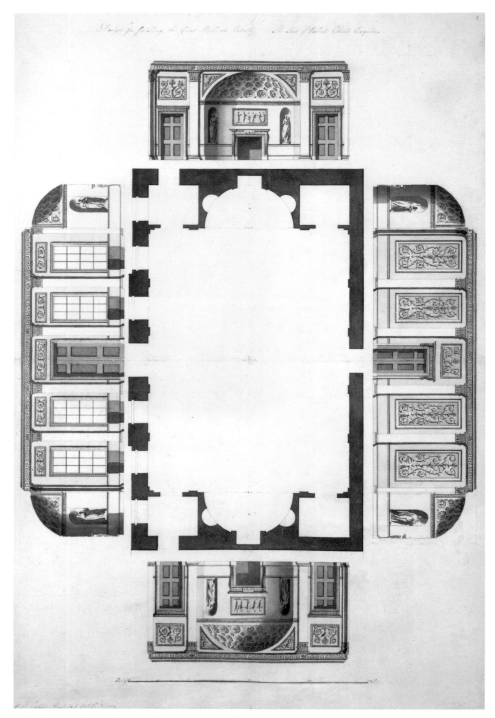

Adam's 1767 design for the Hall (Victoria & Albert Museum)

'The Triumph of Bacchus'; painted grisaille bas-relief by Cipriani above one of the Hall chimney-pieces

north side where there was a secondary hall or vestibule leading to the main staircase. Though this entrance has been removed, the original servants' entrance next to it survives. Special provision was made for serving food and drink in the Hall from behind the door in the north-west corner. This opens to a counter at the head of the circular servants' stair by which food was brought up from the kitchen located in the far distant south-east corner of the house.

STUCCOWORK

The stucco panels of military trophies contribute to the vertical emphasis of the elongated pilasters. Though the much-admired antique marble trophies of Octavianus Augustus on the Campidoglio in Rome were the ultimate source for these, their relationship to the gilded stucco trophies executed a few years earlier and a few miles away in Adam's vestibule at Syon is more immediate. Military trophies – a hangover from the days when arms and armour were regularly hung in great halls – were used again in the hall at Newby in Yorkshire.

Armorial trophies certainly seem more appropriate for a hall than the panels of arabesque ornament shown in Adam's preliminary designs, especially as the adjacent Eating Room had recently been decorated with similar stucco ornaments (see p.50). The arabesque panels over the doors and windows are shown in Adam's original design, except for the painted portrait medallion of Isaac Newton over the door to the Long Gallery, which does not respect the foliate ornament and was an afterthought. Who was responsible for the stucco-work here and elsewhere at Osterley is not known.

DECORATION

The present colour scheme differs in part both from Agneta Yorke's description of it in 1772, when 'the ornaments [were] white and the ground a greenish light grey', and from the 'three tints grey ... minutely disposed' by the painter David Adamson in 1787.

FLOOR

The marble floor with a black pattern on a white ground answers Adam's ceiling in reverse and may also be by him.

CHIMNEY-PIECES

The white marble chimney-pieces, embellished with the Child family crest of an eagle holding an adder in its beak, were designed by Robert Adam in 1768.

PICTURES AND SCULPTURE

ABOVE RIGHT-HAND CHIMNEY-PIECE:

GIOVANNI BATTISTA CIPRIANI (1727–85)
The Triumph of Ceres
Painted grisaille bas-relief
Ceres, goddess of plenty, taught man to till the earth with a plough after the end of the Golden Age.

IN FLANKING NICHES:

Copies of antique sculptures of Ceres and Hercules (holding the golden apples he had seized from the Garden of the Hesperides).

ABOVE LEFT-HAND CHIMNEY-PIECE:

GIOVANNI BATTISTA CIPRIANI (1727–85)
The Triumph of Bacchus
Bacchus taught man to cultivate the vine.

IN FLANKING NICHES:

Statues of Apollo and Minerva, representing poetry and the Arts.

FURNITURE

ON PILASTERS BETWEEN WINDOWS:

A pair of carved brackets supporting vases with branches for three lights. Designed by Adam and originally painted white along with the stuccowork in 1772.

UNDER TROPHIES ON OPPOSITE WALL:

Four 'scroll end stools' by Adam, painted white in 1787.

FLANKING ALCOVES:

Four carved and painted pedestals supporting marble vases with bas-relief figures of bacchanalian children and merfolk. Adam is not known to have designed them. Stylistically, they could date from the late 1750s and may have been made for the earlier hall. The arrangement of the statuary in the new Hall was probably like that at Syon, with the 'reclining Magdalen' and 'Sleeping Jesus' listed in the 1782 inventory placed in front of the alcoves and the four vases and pedestals at the corners of the central rectangle on the marble pavement.

The door to the right of the right-hand alcove leads to the North Vestibule.

THE NORTH VESTIBULE

STUCCOWORK

Adam supplied the stucco decorations.

CERAMICS

IN GLAZED CABINET:

Part of the Childs' large collection of porcelain. Though some of this was originally kept at Osterley, especially in Mrs Child's Dressing Room, the greater part seems to have resided at Berkeley Square and is listed in the 1860 inventory of that house. Especially notable are:

Chelsea mandarin blue tea and coffee service with seated chinoiserie musicians in elaborate gold cartouches on the cups. The fine gilding is attributed to Jenks, a gilder at Chelsea, who is referred to by Josiah Wedgwood in 1765.

Small Sèvres *cabaret* (breakfast or tea service) painted with floral swags enclosing gilt dotted panels, the borders with blue and gilt scale work. The payment to the painter, Guillaume Noel, for overtime work on these pieces in 1766 has been found in the factory records.

Vincennes/Sèvres part *cabaret* painted with birds in gilt flowering cartouches on a *bleu lapis* ground. Decorated in 1756 by Etienne Evans and included in the Berkeley Square inventory.

Vincennes *bleu lapis* cylindrical tankard and cover with gilt panels, marked 1753.

Pear-shaped Sèvres ewer and cover with *beau bleu* ground and gold panels with bouquets of flowers painted by Mereau the Younger. Marked 1765.

THE LIBRARY

This library replaced an earlier one in the centre of the east front, which was demolished when the double portico was created. It was designed by Adam in 1766 to house the 'Entire and Valuable Library' of the late Bryan Fairfax, which had been bought *en bloc* by the young Francis Child ten years earlier. The fine collection of books was Osterley's

The Library in 1926

most distinguished asset, and its sale in 1885 enabled the Jerseys to save the house.

DECORATION

Agneta Yorke was most impressed by the room. 'Mr Adam', she wrote, 'has lavished all his taste in ornamenting every part.' It is stony white and thoroughly architectural, like a classical building turned outside-in. Pedimented Ionic frontispieces with fluted engaged columns accentuate the two large bays facing the windows; the rest are framed by Ionic pilasters enriched with guilloche ornaments. The frieze of circles, bell flowers and rosettes is repeated over the doors, on the two chimney-pieces and around the top of the walls. This was one of Adam's characteristic methods of unifying the diverse elements of a room. The bookcase in the north-east corner is fitted as a jib-door opening to a passage where some of the Ionic cases from the old library are placed.

The paintings, book bindings, four green lute-string (glossy silk) window curtains, green painted Venetian shades with lines and tassels, green cloth covering the desk, and green leather chair cushions were the principal sources of colour.

CEILING

Adam prepared for Child alternative designs for the ceiling from which to choose, one coloured, the other uncoloured. A third design with different colouring is at the Soane Museum. In the late nineteenth and early twentieth centuries the ceiling was green and it was subsequently painted according to the coloured design at Osterley, but recent paint analysis has revealed that it was originally uncoloured, or 'plain white', as Agneta Yorke reported in 1772. A similar monochromatic scheme was used in the hall at Syon and the gallery at Croome Court. This ceiling with its small-scale ornaments and low relief is more characteristic of Adam's work in the late 1760s than the robust Dining Room and Drawing Room ceilings.

PICTURES

The subjects allude, appropriately for the room, to the Arts and Sciences.

FROM OVER DOOR, CLOCKWISE:

ANTONIO ZUCCHI (1726–95)

Britannia encouraging and rewarding Arts and Sciences
Zucchi had been taken up by James Adam in Italy and was persuaded by the Adam brothers to come to England in 1766. From that time until his marriage to Angelica Kauffman and departure in 1781, he was Robert Adam's principal decorative painter.

Plato and his Disciples

Pericles and Socrates listening to Aspasia
Aspasia was the mistress of the Athenian leader Pericles and a noted philosopher.

OVER MANTEL:

GIOVANNI BATTISTA CIPRIANI (1727–85)
Anacreon sacrificing to the Graces
The stucco frame was designed by Adam.

ANTONIO ZUCCHI (1726–95)
Catullus writing an Epitaph for the Death of his Mistress's Bird

The Shipwreck of Aristippus
The Greek philosopher Aristippus and his companions are driven on the shore after being shipwrecked, and by some mathematical lines on the sand know that the land is inhabited.

Pythagoras restoring birds and fishes to their former freedom

Mitellus and Diodorus
Mitellus, a philosopher and general in the Roman army, orders a marble crow for the tomb of his master, Diodorus, because he taught him to chatter and not to reason.

The Muse of Ovid delivering a feather taken from the Wing of Love
Ovid was famous for his love poetry, which included the *Amores* and *Ars Amatoria*.

John Linnell's Library desk is ornamented with inlaid trophies of music and painting

OVER MANTEL:

GIOVANNI BATTISTA CIPRIANI (1727–85)
Sappho writing the Odes dictated by Love

ANTONIO ZUCCHI (1726–95)
Virgil reading his works to Augustus and Octavia
Augustus breaks into tears and Octavia faints when
Virgil recites the passage from the *Aeneid* describing
the death of Octavia's son Marcellus.

*Apollo and Minerva on Mount Parnassus in the
company of the Muses*

FURNITURE

The superb suite of ormolu-mounted marquetry
furniture, every piece decorated with bands of
Vitruvian (wave-like) scrolls, is thought to have
been supplied in 1768 or 1769 by John Linnell. The
remarkably sophisticated French Neo-classical style
of these pieces can be credited to the two young
Swedish cabinetmakers in Linnell's employ at that
time, Christopher Fürlohg and his brother-in-law,
George Haupt. The cost of this furniture must have
been very great, but then, as Agneta Yorke said, 'no
expense has been spared any where'. The suite
consists of:

Eight lyre-back armchairs with ormolu cameos of
classical heads, a different one on each chair.

A pair of library tables almost identical to a pair at
Alnwick Castle.

A large pedestal desk with emblems of architecture,
sculpture, painting and music inlaid on the four
doors.

THE BREAKFAST ROOM

The Breakfast Room has the best view of the park
with its woods and lakes and for that reason was
used as a daytime sitting-room. It was where Sophie
de la Roche, a German visitor who had a ticket to see
the house in 1786, waited for the caretaker to show
her and her party around. The Dowager Duchess of
Cleveland received visitors here when she lived at
Osterley in the 1870s, and the Jerseys thereafter
regularly used it as their family living-room.

DECORATION

The decoration of the room predates Adam's
remodelling and was altered at least once in the
nineteenth century. In 1772 Agneta Yorke men-

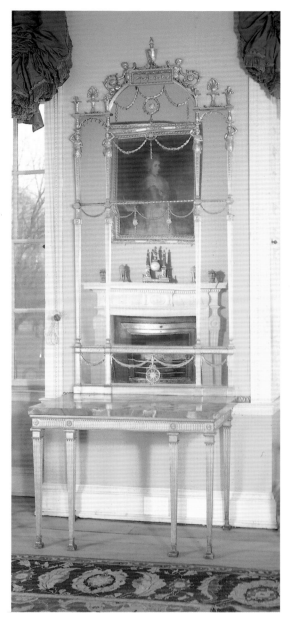

*One of the Adam pier-glasses and tables in the
Breakfast Room*

tioned that the walls were 'Lemon colour with blew ornaments' and were 'hung full of pictures, and the beautiful portrait of Mrs Child, by Cotes is over the Chimney'. According to the 1782 inventory there were 'In all fortyone Pictures in gilt Frames'. (These have now gone.)

CHIMNEY-PIECE

The chimney-piece is probably a post-Adam alteration: the reeding on its frieze and on the dado rail is certainly not characteristic of the 1750s.

FURNITURE

Adam's only contribution to the decoration is the pair of arched pier-glasses subdivided by slender female terms, and the even more streamlined pair of pier-tables. His design at the Soane Museum is dated 24 April 1777.

The suite of ten armchairs and a settee to match is attributed to John Linnell. The lyre-back chairs were bound to attract Agneta Yorke's attention: their upholstery, she wrote, was 'Mrs Child's own work in very elegant frames, in quite a new taste'.

The 'Harpsichord in a mahogany case' listed in the 1782 inventory was a recent addition to the room, having been made in 1781 by the celebrated maker of English harpsichords, Jacob Kirckman, and his nephew Abraham, whose signatures are inscribed on a tablet set into the nameboard. It was probably made for the Child's daughter, Sarah Anne, the favourite pupil of the singer and composer Gabriel Piozzi, who dedicated a set of six sonatas to her. After her death in 1793, her husband, the Earl of Westmorland, must have asked for the harpsichord as a *memento mori*, for it was sent to him in 1795 and returned to Osterley when their daughter, Sarah Sophia, was refurnishing the house in 1805.

THE GREAT STAIR

The principal staircase rises from the ground floor, where there was originally a family entrance and a secondary hall, to the second floor and the bedrooms.

DECORATION

The walls and ceiling were decorated in two stages. The first stage, for which there are no designs, probably dates from 1765 or 1766 and includes the screens of Corinthian columns on the *piano nobile* and Ionic ones on the floor above, as well as the friezes and panels of large-scale stucco ornaments, including ewers and vases emblematic of hospitality.

In 1767 Robert Child decided to sell his house in Lincoln's Inn Fields and move his valuable paintings by Rubens, one of which hung on a ceiling there, to Osterley. Adam's design for a ceiling to receive the picture is dated 1768 and is composed of a central octagonal compartment with smaller and more delicate ornaments than those on the walls.

CEILING PICTURE

After PETER PAUL RUBENS (1577–1640)
The Glorification of the Duke of Buckingham
The Duke is being escorted by Minerva and Mercury to personifications of Virtue and Honour, who await him in a temple. He is offered a garland by the Three Graces, while Envy attempts in vain to pull him down, and a lion challenges him. The original painting was commissioned by Buckingham when he met Rubens in Paris in 1625 and was finished in 1627, only months before his assassination. It was made for his London residence, York House, where it remained until the house was demolished in 1672 and was then taken to Holland. Sir Francis Child the Elder purchased it in 1697 while travelling in the Low Countries. There is a sketch in the National Gallery, but unfortunately the original, with other large paintings from Osterley, was destroyed by fire in Jersey in 1949. A modern copy replaces it.

FURNITURE

A large suite of Chinese black and gold lacquer hall furniture with the Child arms was also brought to Osterley from Lincoln's Inn Fields after it was sold. Some of the chairs, which conveniently furnished the secondary hall, are now on display in the South Passage.

LIGHTING

The Great Stair was lit by three oil lamps in the antique style within glass lanterns that hang between the Corinthian columns on the principal floor. In addition, there is a pair of different lanterns placed on carved and painted wood tripod pedestals with ram's heads. In 1782 one of the pedestals stood

The Great Stair in 1926

on the stairs and the other in the North Passage. The upper part of these standing lanterns is separated from the glass bowl by four dolphins derived from James 'Athenian' Stuart's reconstruction of the lost tripod on the Choragic Monument of Lysicrates illustrated in his *Antiquities of Athens* (1762). Both sets of lanterns are thought to have been made by Matthew Boulton and were published, along with some of the Eating Room furniture at Osterley, in the third, posthumous volume of Adam's *Works in Architecture* (1822), wrongly described as 'Furniture at Sion-house'. (Adam's original designs are lost.) Though their exact date is unknown, it must be before 1772, when the pedestals were painted green and white to match the walls. Another pair of 'green and white painted Terms with bell glasses and lamps' once stood in the vestibule or secondary hall.

STAIRCASE

Adam's designs for the wrought-iron balusters decorated with classical anthemions (honeysuckle) have not survived. They are identical to the balusters made in 1769 for the great stair at Kenwood, and are most likely of the same date. In 1773–4 they were

Adam's satinwood bed with floral silk hangings in the Yellow Taffeta Bedchamber

painted 'fair blue'. The carving of Vitruvian scrolls on the sides of the mahogany banister rail to match the wall moulding is a nice example of Adam's attention to unifying details.

THE YELLOW TAFFETA BEDCHAMBER

When Francis Child had this room remodelled in 1759, it was called 'the first chamber'. It was the principal family bedroom, second only to the master bedroom. In 1786, when Sophie de la Roche visited Osterley, which was then the home of Robert Child's widow, Sarah, this bedroom and its dressing-room 'with hangings of East India Material' were the apartments of Sarah's daughter and her husband, the Earl of Westmorland. Though the bedrooms at Osterley may seem empty in comparison with the Child's living- and reception-rooms, that is how they were in the eighteenth century.

CHIMNEY-PIECE

The 1759 remodelling by Matthew Hillyard reused some old material, and introduced a new wood chimney-piece probably made by William Linnell or his son John from a design by William Chambers. The chimney-piece frieze is carved with a central anthemion flanked by scrolling foliage, and is supported by scroll trusses ornamented with laurel wreaths and interlaced foliage emerging from vases resting on draped female masks.

BED

In 1779 Robert Child had John Linnell refurnish the room with a suite of satinwood furniture. There is a design by Adam at the Soane Museum dated 10 April 1779 for the bed, which has a cavetto (concave) cornice of satinwood veneer, inlaid with green-stained wood, and surmounted by carved and gilt putti flanking a wreathed vase and anthemion. The window cornices were evidently made from the same design. Less costly painted decoration was applied to the partly concealed satinwood bed posts.

The bed-hangings and window curtains are of pale yellow taffeta painted with an oriental floral design and embellished with green silk festoons, fringes and tassels. They were remade in the 1920s. The 'Silk Shade', or protective curtain, which was lowered when the bed was not in use, has not survived, nor has the counterpane, which was described in the 1782 inventory as of 'rich Satin Decca work lined and fringed'. Decca work (embroidery made in the Deccan in southern India) was imported into this country in large quantities in the late seventeenth and eighteenth centuries. A surviving example of it can be seen on the bed valance in Mr Child's Bedroom (see p.49).

OTHER FURNITURE

The remainder of the furniture was designed by Linnell himself and made to match the bed. The inventory lists 'Nine Elbow Satinwood Chairs inlaid and Japanned Cane seats Cushions covered with Taffety fringed', two satinwood veneered night tables cross-banded with rosewood, a satinwood pembroke table, a small oval satinwood table and a deal toilet table elaborately dressed with a 'quilted Stuff coat with gold worked muslin cover of Silk Veil covered with ditto'. The two latter pieces do not survive, nor do the carpets placed before the toilet table and round the bed. The splat-back chairs are not really satinwood, but painted to simulate it and inlaid with green-stained wood. The satinwood chest of drawers *en suite* with the night tables is not in the inventory and was evidently made after 1782.

The gilt frames for the pier-glass and the Chinese overmantel picture painted on glass have central anthemion ornaments and scrolled foliage corresponding to the frieze on the chimney-piece. They probably date from around 1760.

The 'Taffety Dressing Room', which served this bedroom, no longer exists. It had curtains of the same painted satin Decca work as the counterpane, and four armchairs identical to those in the bedroom.

MR CHILD'S DRESSING ROOM

The Childs' private apartment begins to the left at the head of the Great Stair with Mr Child's Dressing Room and Bedroom. These interconnecting rooms were refurbished for Francis Childs in 1759 by Matthew Hillyard, who made the friezes and put up the doors and shutters, incorporating old materials wherever possible. The door surrounds, for example, date from the late seventeenth century, when the house was improved by Dr Nicholas Barbon. The room seems to have been altered in the late nineteenth century, when the built-in corner cupboard was added.

CHIMNEY-PIECE

The chimney-piece may also date from the late nineteenth century. It is identical to the one in the bedroom and one would not expect to find the same design so exactly repeated in two different rooms in the eighteenth century. The quality of the copy is so high that it is virtually indistinguishable from its model.

FURNITURE

Nothing remains of the furniture made for Mr Child's Dressing Room, which, according to the inventory, included blue 'lustring [glossy silk] festoon window Curtains' and a blue Brussels carpet, an oval pier-glass in a carved and painted frame, a mahogany wardrobe with drawers, shelves and wire door with blue silk behind, a mahogany shaving stand and commode, and a horse picture over the chimney-piece.

DRAWINGS

Around the walls are photographic reproductions of most of the presentation designs made by Adam for Francis and Robert Child. Other drawings for the decoration, furniture and garden buildings at Osterley are in the Adam volumes at Sir John Soane's Museum.

CERAMICS

IN GLASS-FRONTED CABINETS:

Part of a Chinese armorial dinner service with the coat of arms of the Childs of Worcester and London, granted on 28 January 1701. This service is the only known one with a powder-blue border and was almost certainly made in the early 1720s for Sir Francis Child the Younger. It is thought to have been commissioned at the same time as the armorial lacquer furniture and, like it, was probably destined for Child's house in Lincoln's Inn Fields. The service was enlarged by the Jerseys in the 1820s with excellent pieces made to match, including the ice pails and entrée dishes displayed here. Also shown are plates from the Jersey Meissen dinner service.

MR CHILD'S BEDROOM

This room is more intact than the ancillary Dressing Room. It was decorated for the bachelor Francis Child and then used by Robert and Sarah Child.

CHIMNEY-PIECE

In about 1759 a design for a chimney-piece was obtained by the surveyor in charge of the work, Boulton Mainwaring, from William Chambers, possibly via Joseph Wilton, who also procured designs from him for the Long Gallery chimney-pieces. The design was most likely executed by William or John Linnell, who supplied the chimney-piece and most of the furniture in Mrs Child's Dressing Room next door and in the Yellow Taffeta Bedchamber.

FURNITURE

The only pieces of original furniture here are the mahogany four-poster bed, the large seventeenth-century French ebony cabinet and the Chinese lacquer chest of drawers. The bed was once completely furnished with hangings, valances and a counterpane of embroidered Indian silk. This has all perished except for the valances and bed cornices. There are also matching festoon window curtains, and chair covers for a suite of 'Six Mahogany Back Stool Chairs' that has not survived. The missing chairs, the 'Pier Glass in a rich Carved and gilt frame fifty six and a half by forty inches', the mahogany night table and mahogany pot cupboard listed in the inventory have been replaced by other furniture, including the remainder of the set of Linnell chairs in the Yellow Taffeta Bedchamber and the bed-steps, which were supplied for the State Bed-chamber in the 1880s.

The door to the right of the bed leads to Mr Child's Dressing Room and that on the opposite wall to Mrs Child's two closets and Dressing Room.

MRS CHILD'S DRESSING ROOM

In 1782 this was 'Mrs Child's Dressing Room', her principal dressing-room or boudoir. Sarah Child presumably used the room primarily as a boudoir for ladies to retire to. All her paraphernalia for dressing – dressing-tables and stools, a wardrobe,

The Indian embroidered silk hangings in Mr Child's Bedroom

'cut bottles', boxes and trays, dressing glasses – and eleven more paintings were in the two adjoining closets, one of these (which is now a bathroom) being in the turret. She had another, smaller 'Dressing Room' in the south-east corner of the house above the kitchen, which, judging from its mahogany library table and 'Secretaire with Doors, Draws and rising top' listed in the inventory, she used as an office. When the present Lord Jersey lived at Osterley, this was his bedroom, with the bed placed against the north wall and a door beside it leading to the dressing-room and closet in the passage and turret respectively.

DECORATION

The shutters with octagonal panels and the frieze were put up in the 1750s. The date of the other decoration is not at all certain. If the chimney-piece was part of the work carried out for Mrs Sarah Child, then its date would have to be after October 1763, when she married Robert Child and he inherited the house – probably around 1765 or 1766. However, it is hard to believe that such a full blown and outmoded Rococo chimney-piece would have been put up when Adam was in full swing, even in a private, lady's apartment. Possibly it was made around 1762 in anticipation of Francis Child's marriage; it could also have been made in the 1750s for Agatha, wife of Samuel Child (who died in 1752) and mother of Francis and Robert. The door surrounds are probably early twentieth-century. The wallpaper has been painted to match traces of blue paint found behind the chimney-piece.

49

John Linnell's carved wood chimney-piece in Mrs Child's Dressing Room

CHIMNEY-PIECE

The chimney-piece was made by John Linnell of carved wood and painted white to accord with the marble inset. His design for the gilt overmantel incorporates brackets for the display of porcelain and a portrait. The present portrait is said to be of Sarah Anne Child, who was born in 1764; if so, it must have been inserted in the 1770s in place of an earlier portrait.

FURNITURE

Seventeenth-century Japanese lacquer cabinet on an early eighteenth-century stand. This is the only item surviving from the 1770s.

None of the furniture in the 1782 inventory is in the room now. This included a pair of 'Glass bordered pier Glasses in gilt frames' which can be identified

with a pair of carved and gilt Rococo pier-glasses with shell crests in Lord Jersey's possession. Under them was a pair of 'inlaid commodes with ormolu ornaments', also belonging to Lord Jersey, and almost certainly by Linnell. There was also 'a very Elegant Gilt Cabinet with thick carved and Gilt door with plate glass on a rich carved frame containing various India and other Curiosities', eight green and gold cabriole chairs covered with satin, a small table inlaid with ivory, a mahogany sliding firescreen and thirteen paintings. Walpole reported that 'Mrs Child's dressing-room [was] full of pictures, gold filigree, china and japan. So is all the house . . .'

THE EATING ROOM

In his *Works in Architecture* (1772) Adam described English eating-rooms as:

apartments of conversation, in which we are to pass a great deal of our time. This renders it desirable to have them fitted up with elegance and splendour, but in a style different from that of other apartments. Instead of being hung with damask, tapestry &c. they are always finished with stucco, and adorned with statues and paintings, that they may not retain the smell of the victuals.

Though the room faces north, its colouring and view of the flower garden make it one of the most cheerful rooms in the house.

DECORATION

The cavetto cornice of intertwined grape vines, which is omitted from Adam's design and does not match his door architraves, most likely belongs to Hillyard's 1756–9 refurbishment. 1766 is the earliest date we have for Adam's work in this room. It strongly suggests that the ceiling, which would have been attended to first and well before any furniture, dates from 1765 or even earlier and was closely followed by the undated design for the walls. Adam also designed the curtain cornices.

The close relationship between this room and the dining-room designed by Adam in 1761 for William Drake at Shardeloes in Buckinghamshire was evidently desired by both clients and dutifully forged by their mutual architect. Left to his own devices, Adam did not as a rule repeat his designs as exactly as he did in these two houses.

The Eating Room

CEILING

Decorated with grape vines, thyrsi (ivy-wreathed staves), wine ewers and other Bacchic emblems appropriate to an eating room, it is virtually identical to the one executed by Joseph Rose at Shardeloes before February 1763.

PICTURES

OVER SIDEBOARD:

ANTONIO ZUCCHI (1726–95)
Turkish figures dancing among classical ruins

OPPOSITE:

Figures sporting in a ruined Roman bath
These classical *capricci* were executed in 1767 in the style of Charles-Louis Clérisseau, who was artistic tutor to the Adam brothers while they were in Italy, and visited London in 1766, shortly after painting a 'ruin room' at S. Trinità dei Monti, Rome.

OVER DOORS:

The four known Continents

RECTANGULAR TABLETS WITHIN STUCCO PANELS:

Festive scenes of nymphs with satyrs
According to classical legend, satyrs were responsible for the education of Bacchus.

ROUNDELS WITHIN STUCCO PANELS:

A Roman marriage

A wedding feast

The birth of a baby

The sacrifice of a ram in thanksgiving

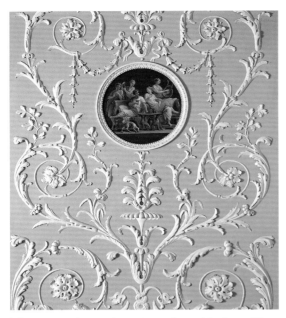

The stucco arabesque decoration and roundel of a wedding feast by Antonio Zucchi in the Eating Room

OVER CHIMNEY-PIECE:

GIOVANNI BATTISTA CIPRIANI (1727–85)
An offering to Ceres
Women and children offer sacrifices to a statue of Ceres, goddess of plenty, and sing her praises to the accompaniment of a lyre.

DOORS

For the sake of symmetry, the room has four doors: the pair to the door from the Long Gallery is false and the servants' entrance, which is the pair to the door from the North Passage, was found bolted by the present Lord Jersey. He had it reopened (as it must have been originally) to allow direct access to the back stair from which food was brought up from the kitchen located in the south-east corner of the house. Behind this door is an ingenious tray-table that slides up into the soffit of the door when not needed.

CHIMNEY-PIECE

The chimney-piece is not only remarkably large, 6 feet 3 inches tall and 7 feet 7 inches wide, but the use of the Doric order, normally reserved for halls, is also unusual. As it appears in Adam's wall elevation,

albeit somewhat smaller and simpler, there is no reason to doubt that it was designed by him.

FURNITURE

Visitors entering the Eating Room from the Long Gallery were bound to be as impressed as Agneta Yorke was by Adam's carved and gilt mahogany sideboard, 'Magnificently furnishd with plate, and under the Table was a Massy & large silver Cistern', reminding them of the fact that the Childs were goldsmith bankers and extremely rich. The sideboard, designed in 1767, has unusually complex tapered and spiral-fluted legs, and a Greek-key frieze incorporating *paterae* (circular ornaments) and *bucrania* (ox skulls) related to the Doric chimney-piece.

FLANKING TABLE:

A pair of round, fluted pedestals painted white and partly gilt, surmounted by carved mahogany vases, one of which is lined with lead to hold water. The bases were probably fitted out like those at Sharde-loes, one to hold the chamberpot and the other a mahogany pail. An engraving of the sideboard, pedestal and vase, erroneously described as 'Furni-ture at Sion-house', was published after Adam's death in the third volume of his *Works* (1822).

BETWEEN WINDOWS:

En suite pier-tables, with the same frieze as the sideboard but simpler legs, which were needed to support their heavy 'antique' marble mosaic slabs.

ABOVE PIER-TABLES:

Oval pier-glasses, 4 feet 8 inches tall and just over 3 feet wide, in gilt frames surmounted by ornamental hanging devices over $7\frac{1}{2}$ feet tall. These mirrors are more ornate than the ones shown in Adam's wall elevation. The design for them at the Soane Museum is dated 1767. Their heaviness is in pro-portion to the outsize chimney-piece, the very large paintings and the robustness of the stucco decorations.

AGAINST WALLS:

Twelve mahogany chairs with lyre backs and two armchairs with backs and seats upholstered in red leather. In the eighteenth century dining-chairs were always kept in the room, but placed against the walls when not in use. The lyre-back chairs were designed by Adam and almost certainly made by Linnell, who is also credited with the rest of the

Adam's engraving of the Eating Room sideboard, pedestals and vases

Eating Room furniture. The 'charming harmony' between the lyre backs 'taken from antique lyres' and the scrolled foliage in the antique style struck a chord with Walpole. French interest in the ancient lyre both as a musical instrument and as a decorative motif in the early 1760s is thought to have inspired the English development of the lyre-back chair, which only later became popular in France.

Dining-tables were kept in the passage and only brought into the room when needed. In 1782 there were three small tables in the North Passage and two sets of four large ones with rounded ends in the South Passage.

CARPET

The carpet was rewoven by the Victoria & Albert Museum following the late nineteenth-century copy of the eighteenth-century original.

THE GALLERY

This room, 130 feet long, occupies the whole length of the garden front. It was refurbished in 1756–9 as a gallery for the Childs' large collection of pictures. After 1764 Adam filled in the Venetian windows that had been inserted in the end walls in 1759 and hung pea-green wallpaper.

The Gallery was very different in the early nineteenth century, when Sarah Sophia, Countess of Jersey lived here. It was filled with furniture, including a billiard table and pianoforte, and used as a drawing-room. An American visitor, Louis Simon, noted 'tables, sofas and chairs . . . studiously *derangés* about the fire-places and in the middle of the room, as if the family had just left them, such is the modern fashion of placing furniture carried to an extreme.' Henry James summed it up as 'a cheerful upholstered avenue into another century'.

In the late nineteenth and early twentieth centuries Margaret, Lady Jersey gave legendary receptions in this room, which was lit by 400 candles, some placed over the shuttered windows.

DECORATION

The 1756–9 work was carried out by Matthew Hillyard. Though extremely wealthy, the Childs were not extravagant. Old joinery was reused and new made to match; as a result it is now extremely difficult to date things accurately. Much remains of the old work here, including the large Ionic doorcase in the centre and four smaller ones at the ends. These were all copied from an engraving of Charles I's chapel at Somerset House, published in 1731 in Isaac Ware's *Designs of Inigo Jones*, and probably date from the later 1730s or early '40s, when a great deal of work was being done at Osterley. The bold foliate frieze incorporating marigolds, the symbol of Child's Bank, could also have been made in the 1740s, but would have been painted white and not picked out.

It seems, from surviving building accounts and from Adam's rejected design of 1761, that at least one of the doors and the two fireplaces were moved when the new Hall was formed in 1764.

CHIMNEY-PIECES

The marble chimney-pieces were executed with modifications from a design (in the Avery Library, New York) by the architect William Chambers. The drawing was obtained around 1759 not by Francis Child or his clerk of works, Boulton Mainwaring, but by Joseph Wilton, the sculptor who was contracted to supply them. The chimney-pieces may have been finished by 1761, but the readjusted fireplaces were not ready to receive them until 1764, by which time Adam was in full control.

PICTURES

OVER CHIMNEY-PIECES:

After ANTHONY DEVIS (1729–1817)
Osterley from the south-east
Painted in 1784.

After ANTHONY DEVIS (1729–1817)
Osterley from the south-west
Painted in 1784.

The other paintings are on loan from the Victoria & Albert Museum and the Royal Collection, and are not indigenous to the house.

MIRRORS

Although the Gallery was regarded as 'built' when Adam arrived on the scene in 1761 and was not his concern, he was called upon to design pier-glasses for the room after the success of the mirrors he had created for Child's house in Berkeley Square in 1769 and 1770. A rejected design made in 1768 for the Earl of Shelburne at Lansdowne House was used to frame the four large pier-glasses. According to

One of the gilt girandoles in the Gallery

Agneta Yorke, these mirrors were purchased by Mr Child at Gunnersbury, probably before Princess Amelia, George II's sister, bought the house in 1762, and were 'larger than those in his House in Town'.

Evidently the six large girandoles with unusual heart-shaped glasses were not up in 1772, or Mrs Yorke would surely have commented upon them. Their carved and gilt frames formed of foliate branches with female terms at the sides and festoons of husks criss-crossed over the glass are closely related to mirrors designed by Adam in 1768 for Coventry House, Piccadilly. They were almost certainly made by John Linnell.

OTHER FURNITURE

Linnell is also credited with the earlier suite of twelve mahogany armchairs and six settees with seat rails matching the dado rail and straight fluted legs echoing motifs found on Chambers's chimney-pieces. The two long settees placed against the end walls were added after 1764, when the Venetian windows were removed. They were reupholstered in 1888–9 with the embroidered sign of Child's Bank on one, and the Jersey arms on the other. Originally the suite was covered with 'pea Green silk and Stuff Damask' to match the paper on the walls.

The 1782 inventory also listed a suite of 24 green and white cabriole chairs with cane seats and backs, known as rout chairs. Though they belonged to the room, they were probably kept in the passage and turret room and brought out when needed. Amidst the profusion of seat furniture, there was only one small mahogany table and two mahogany flower stands placed in front of the windows in 1782. The mid-eighteenth-century Chinese imperial junks have also been at Osterley since at least 1782; the dragon represents the emperor, the phoenix the empress. The pair of Chinese pagodas is of a similar date.

CERAMICS

When Sophie de la Roche was conducted round the house in 1786, she noted 'tremendous Japanese vases' in the Gallery. These were not in the room four years earlier, when the inventory was made, and were probably brought here from Berkeley Square. The two pairs of Chinese *famille rose* mandarin jars and the pair of *famille rose* blue ground mandarin vases were made in the early part of the reign of the Chinese emperor Qianlong (1736–95).

THE DRAWING ROOM

This room balances the Eating Room at the opposite end of the Gallery. Adam probably began work on both of them for Robert Child in 1765 or 1766, though it is possible that the scheme was conceived as early as 1763 for Francis Child.

CEILING

The ceiling is modelled on the ancient Temple of the Sun published in Robert Wood's *Ruins of Palmyra* (1753). However, the immediate inspiration is the *trompe-l'oeil* Palmyra ceiling in the nave of West Wycombe church, painted for Sir Francis Dashwood, Lord Le Despencer by Giuseppe Mattia Borgnis, whose son, Pietro Maria, was responsible for painting the ornaments in the Etruscan Dressing Room. Borgnis's ceiling in the hall at Dashwood's house, West Wycombe Park, is even more closely related to Osterley, but its date is uncertain and may be as late as 1770. Dashwood's brother-in-law, John Walcot, secured Samuel and Francis Child's seats in Parliament (see p.16) and it was most likely Dashwood himself who recommended Robert Adam to Francis Child.

The presence of two ceilings with Buckinghamshire prototypes – one in the Eating Room and the other in the Drawing Room – cannot be mere coincidence. The idea was certainly more meaningful to the Childs than to Adam and is more likely to be theirs than his. Adam never used the Temple of the Sun model again.

In order to fit the Palmyra ceiling to the rectangular shape of the Drawing Room, Adam replaced the circular centre with an oval, and added a single row of coffers all round. This addition does not appear in his design, which adheres exactly to the coffering pattern of the original engraved model, increasing the size of the coffers rather than the number to fill the space. The large coffers were evidently abandoned as being too bold for the room; even the smaller coffering that was executed is somewhat heavy, especially in relation to the lighter treatment of the frieze, the doorcases and chimney-piece.

CARPET

The carpet was designed by Adam in 1774 to answer the ceiling. It has a similar pattern composed of circles instead of octagons, inspired by another plate

The Drawing Room

in Wood's *Palmyra*. It was made by Thomas Moore (*c.*1700–88) of Moorfields.

FRIEZE AND WALL-COVERINGS

Adam's undated design for the four walls shows a frieze of scrolled foliage, a standard classical motif that was also used in West Wycombe church and many other places. The motif is repeated in the frieze over the doors where it is interrupted by a central tablet containing a profile medallion flanked by griffins.

The room was painted by David Adamson in 1772, at which time the 'old frieze and architrave' was 'taken down' and replaced by the present one, which has a repeating pattern of arcades incorporating anthemion and bell flowers picked out in gold on a dark crimson ground. Contrary to Adam's

normal practice of linking the various elements of his decorative scheme, this frieze bears no relation to any of the architectural components. There is, however, an almost identical frieze associated with the painted Palmyra ceiling in the hall at West Wycombe Park which is said to date from 1770 or shortly after. Again the similarity cannot be mere coincidence.

Dark crimson seems to have been an uncommon colour for a frieze, and Walpole made special note of the 'admirable effect' it had with the 'pale green damask' hangings, described by Agneta Yorke as 'pea green'. The damask was last replaced in the late nineteenth-century. The need for a bold and distinctive accent here may have arisen in 1772 in relation to the novel plans then being formulated for the adjacent State Apartment.

(Right) The Drawing Room ceiling

Adam's 1774 design for the Drawing Room carpet (Victoria & Albert Museum)

FIREPLACE

The chimney-piece is oddly disparate and was redesigned to match the doors, though in execution the griffins were superseded by sphinxes.

Adam's gold-coloured grate and fender, echoing the scrolled foliage on the chimney-piece and the arcaded enrichment of the wall frieze, were part of the 1773 smartening up of the room. They are made of paktong, an alloy of copper, zinc and nickel. The semi-circular cast-iron fireback with arcaded edging was initially intended to have a figured medallion like the painted one proposed for the side of the commode, but was modified in execution. This is the only Adam grate that remains *in situ*.

FURNITURE

The suite of eight carved and gilt armchairs and two sofas with Rococo shell ornaments and cabriole legs was designed and made by John Linnell around 1769, at the same time as the Neo-classical Library furniture. The combination of Neo-classical decoration and Rococo furniture was perfectly acceptable to the taste of the time. Both styles were fashionable and that is what mattered, not their differences. The suite was covered with the same pea-green silk damask as once covered the walls; it was re-covered in the 1970s.

The pair of bow-fronted commodes was designed by Adam in January 1773 with figured roundels in the centre and on the sides, a frieze to match the doorcases, and an arcaded base corresponding to the frieze round the room. These commodes have no function; they are ornamental wall decorations and were initially intended to be painted or at least to have painted tops. In the event, they were veneered with hardwood, satinwood and other woods, some stained green, and mounted with ormolu. Linnell is thought to have supplied the hollow cases and the Swedish cabinetmaker Christopher Fürlohg the marquetry roundels. An alternative attribution to Ince and Mayhew has been suggested on the basis of similarities to their Derby House commode. The roundels depicting *Diana and her hounds* and *Venus explaining the torch of Hymen to Cupid* were taken from engravings after paintings by Angelica Kauffman. The oval medallions on the sides feature bacchantes or festive female figures inspired partly by antique gems and wall paintings.

The accompanying pier-glasses, 8 foot 3 inches by 4 foot 4 inches, were too large to be made in this country and had to be imported from France. Their frames, for which there is a design by Adam dated 21 July 1773, have crests of seated female figures, a motif first used in 1771 in a design for a chimney-glass for Child's back drawing-room at Berkeley Square. Contrary to normal practice, the bases of these frames were omitted and their remaining borders made narrower than usual so as to add to the continuity and the apparent height of the decoration of the piers. It seems, however, that this novel arrangement was not entirely satisfactory, for in August 1783 Linnell supplied '2 Pieces of fine Brass Wire Work in brass Molding frames to stand before the Glasses'. They have since disappeared.

The two tripods are Adam-style candlestands of carved and gilt wood, nearly six feet tall, embellished with ram's heads similar to those under the brackets of the chimney-piece and door architraves. These are not listed in the inventory and may have come from Berkeley Square. The candlebranches they were made to support, may originally have been at Berkeley Square or Upton and have been identified with a payment to Matthew Boulton in 1772.

The carved and gilt 'pole fire screen covered with Needlework' in the inventory is not known to have been designed by Adam, though it is in his style. It is embroidered with love-birds.

One of the ormolu and marquetry commodes designed by Adam in 1773 for the Drawing Room

VASES

The mantelpiece was a showcase for Robert Child's impressive collection of ormolu-mounted spar vases made by Matthew Boulton. 'Two Elegant spar Vases mounted in Or Molee with double branches and Statuary Pedestals . . . Four spar vases mounted with Or Molee One Spar Vase elegantly mounted on a double Pedestal with Or Molee' are listed in the inventory taken in 1782. The two spar vases with double branches on the mantelpiece may be identified with the pair of bluejohn wing-figured vases without pedestals (the white statuary marble pedestals being extraneous) bought by Child in April 1772 for £29 8s. The four spar vases and one on a double pedestal, presumably meaning a pedestal in two stages separated by ormolu figures like the sphinx vases in the Royal Collection, have not been identified. Child's patronage of Boulton leads one to wonder whether he also commissioned him to make the ormolu door furniture for Osterley to Adam's designs.

PICTURES

In Robert Child's time the Drawing Room walls were hung with eleven Old Master paintings, including a large Ruisdael landscape over the chimney-piece and landscapes by Salvator Rosa and Gaspar Poussin over the four doors. Most of these were replaced in the nineteenth century by family portraits centring around Sarah Sophia, Countess of Jersey, whose youthful portrait by Romney hung over the mantelpiece.

THE TAPESTRY ROOM

This is the first room of the State Apartment designed by Adam for Robert Child. Walpole thought this room 'the most superb and beautiful that can be imagined'.

CEILING

The ceiling as usual was designed first, in 1772, at the same time as the one in the Etruscan Dressing Room. Its central medallion depicts *The dedication of a child to Minerva* (perhaps a pun on the family name); the smaller medallions are of female figures representing the Liberal Arts. These, along with the borders round the circle and four quadrants, were painted on paper, laid down on canvas and fixed in the stucco frames after the ceiling itself was painted in July 1775.

TAPESTRIES

The set of Boucher medallion tapestries, *Tentures de Boucher*, was ordered from Jacques Neilson, *entrepreneur* of the Gobelins factory in Paris and a Scot by origin, around 1772. It corresponds exactly to one executed in 1775–6 '*pour un seigneur anglais*' and was delivered in July 1776. Three other Adam patrons already had similar sets: the Earl of Coventry at Croome Court, Sir Lawrence Dundas at Moor Park in Hertfordshire, and William Weddell at Newby. In this case, unlike the others, the idea was almost certainly initiated by Adam rather than his patron, and was prompted by the installation of the Croome Court tapestry room with its matching furniture in June 1771.

The medallions of Child's set represent the Four Elements as personified by the Loves of the Gods, with the pier-glass taking the place of water. They were designed by the painter François Boucher (1703–70), who was *inspecteur* at the Gobelins factory from 1755, and consist of:

OVER CHIMNEY-PIECE:

Cupid and Psyche
Prominently signed and dated *Neilson ex 1775*. The story is taken from Apuleius's romance, *The Golden Ass*, and shows Psyche about to wake Cupid by spilling oil from her lamp on his wing. It was a popular subject for decorating bedrooms and boudoirs. Flanking it are smaller medallions of cupids.

OPPOSITE:

Venus and Vulcan (Fire)
Venus visits Vulcan in his forge.

FACING WINDOWS:

Aurora and Cephalus (Air)
The dawn goddess Aurora discovers the hunter Cephalus.

Vertumnus and Pomona (Earth)
Pomona, goddess of gardens and orchards, is wooed by Vertumnus, god of spring, who, according to Ovid's *Metamorphoses*, assumed the guise of an old lady in order to sing his own praises.

All are on a *rose damas cramoisy* ground simulating damask. Their oval medallion frames are more classical than earlier sets, as are the new Louis XVI

The Tapestry Room ceiling

architectural borders, which support a variety of birds and animals appropriate to Mrs Child's celebrated menagerie (see p.74). Pieces of tapestry of the same design were used to cover the chimney-board and fire-screen.

CAMEO DECORATION

Adam was criticised by Walpole for sticking 'diminutive heads in bronze no bigger than a half-crown, into the chimney-piece's hair'. However,

the only gilt cameo heads are in the lozenge frieze on the walls. The similar cameos over the doors are of painted plaster and those on the chimney-piece are inlaid coloured scagliola, sometimes called 'Bossi work' after an Italian craftsman of that name active in Dublin, who specialised in the technique.

FURNITURE

The sofa and eight armchairs are upholstered in *rose damas cramoisy* tapestry to match the walls, with Boucher's *Jeux d'Enfants* in oval frames on the backs and floral compositions designed by Maurice

61

Jacques and Louis Tessier on the seats and arm rests. The cartoons for the *Enfants* were made exclusively for Madame de Pompadour in 1751–3 and returned to Boucher. Their use for other clients was only authorised after her death in 1770. The carved and gilt chair frames were probably designed and made by Linnell shortly after the delivery of the tapestries.

The 'rich Carved and gilt Eliptic Pier Table' has three painted plaques on the rail, corresponding to the inlaid scagliola ones on the chimney-piece, and a statuary marble slab with scagliola ornaments related both to the ceiling and the carpet. It was designed in March 1775.

The design for the accompanying pier-glass frame, dated 28 November 1775, could not have been made until Adam had seen a detailed sketch of the piece of tapestry at the top of the pier or even the piece itself. Only then would he have been able to design a compatible crest consisting of a pedestal and *tazza* of flowers flanked by two standing female figures holding garlands that appear to emerge from the tapestry.

In November 1776, after the tapestries had been put up, Adam designed a pair of unusual tripod pedestals combining pierced, painted, carved and gilt panels enriched with sphinxes, garlands, vases and other ornaments seen in the room. On them stand 'two very elegant Or Molee Vases and Pedestals which carry two lights each'. These have been identified with the pair of wing-figured vases with white bodies on pedestals which Child bought for £37 16s from Matthew Boulton in April 1772. They were the most expensive of Child's several purchases from Boulton in that year and are the

The Tapestry Room

The State Bedchamber ceiling

only known examples of the new wing-figured vases introduced by Boulton in 1772.

CARPET

Neilson supplied Child with a drawing of the principal *tenture* with two medallions, and this must have been used by Adam in July 1775, when he designed the carpet, which is mainly related to the ceiling but also incorporates large baskets of flowers corresponding to the flower vases in the tapestries. The carpet was made by Thomas Moore.

THE STATE BEDCHAMBER

When Mrs Lybbe Powys visited Osterley in 1788, this room was 'call'd the English bed-chamber, as all the furniture is English'. Furniture is certainly the focus of attention, and the ceiling and wall decorations that dominate other rooms are subservient here.

CEILING

The green painted ceiling gives the overall theme – the pleasures of love and nature. The central medallion was inspired by Angelica Kauffman's painting of Aglaia, one of the Three Graces and a nature goddess, being enslaved by Love. The smaller, surrounding paintings, attributed to Zucchi and depicting the pleasures of the pastoral life, were taken from Torquato Tasso's *Gerusaleme Liberata* (1580–1).

MIRRORS

Though the bed is the principal object, it did not have priority in the design sequence. Frames for the very large and costly pier-glasses imported from France were evidently considered more urgent. Designs for the one in this room and the Etruscan Dressing Room were made on 15 May 1775 with similar crests of mirror glass in the shape of pedestals with ram's heads, incorporating roundels. There was no such urgency for the chimney-glass, which has a smaller plate and was one of the first to be made in England, adding substance to the room's 'English' sobriquet. Adam's design, dated 24 April 1777, is taken from the centre part of the chimney-glass in the Etruscan Dressing Room at Derby House, which he designed in 1774 and published in his *Works* in 1779.

STATE BED

A *Design of a Bed for Robert Child Esqr* in the Soane Museum, dated 16 May 1776, corresponds to the bedstead as executed, with its 'Eight painted & Japanned Columns with Carved and gilt Capitals and bases on Inlaid Pedestals', its 'rich Carved and Gilt Cornice' with sphinxes at the projecting corners, its domed tester, and 'Japanned and highly gilt headboard' with nymphs, garlands, putti and dolphins, all attributes of love and fertility. Adam also provided designs for the embroidered silk counterpane and the interior of the dome. The fluid plan – a rectangle with corner projections enclosing a circle (representing the dome) – can be seen in relation both to the central feature of many Adam ceilings of this period, including those in the Tapestry Room and Etruscan Dressing Room, and to the supposed plan of the Temple of the Sun at Baalbec.

Four-poster beds (in this case, actually eight-poster) lend themselves to architectural treatment, but nowhere is this more fully and successfully exploited than at Osterley. The domed structure resembles a temple to the fertility goddesses Venus and Pomona, and celebrates the posterity of the Child family. There is an abundance of painted, stuccoed, carved and embroidered flowers, including the classical anthemion and palmette, which are also used on the wall and door friezes and on the ceiling; rosettes and bell flowers, which are repeated on the bed carpet; marigolds emblematic of Child's Bank alternating on the valance with the Childs' crest of an eagle holding an adder in its beak, and reappearing on the curtain cornices between poppy heads referring to sleep. The silk flower garlands round the dome were remade by Lucy Henderson in the 1980s.

The incongruity of dressing such a distinctly architectural edifice in flowers made the bed an object of ridicule for Walpole. It is, he wrote, 'too theatric and too like a modern head-dress, for round the outside of the dome are festoons of artificial flowers. What would Vitruvius think of a dome decorated by a milliner.' Walpole may not have been aware of the actual theatrical relationship between the dome of the bed and a contemporary design by Adam for a canopied box for George III at the Italian Theatre in Haymarket.

The remarkable survival of the richly embroidered satin counterpane and velvet hangings must owe a great deal to the provision of a silk shade to throw over the bed, Venetian blinds as well as curtains to keep out light, and the painstaking practice of taking down and cleaning the bed every winter when the family was not in residence. The counterpane embroidery was reapplied to new silk *c.*1982.

CARPET

The bed carpet was made by Thomas Moore from an Adam design of February 1779.

WALL-COVERINGS

The predominance of green, a colour allied with fertility and traditionally preferred for bedrooms, is appropriate, though the velvet originally used to cover the walls was perceived by Walpole to be an attribute of winter rather than spring. In the late nineteenth century the deep and soothing velvet was replaced with pleated silk which created quite a different effect. The present material was put up in the 1950s.

SPHINX DECORATION

The winged female sphinxes that inhabit this room are emblems of the *soleil nocturn* and thus of eternal light. They are found on the ceiling, the bed, the pier-glass, on the chimney-board and the suite of six

Adam's 1776 design for the State Bed (Sir John Soane's Museum)

The State Bedchamber

cabriole armchairs designed in April 1777. Their use to support the oval chair backs is completely novel. As the chairs were meant to stand against the wall, the sphinxes are carved only on the front.

CHIMNEY-BOARD

Though the painted chimney-board designed by Adam in 1778 contains motifs found elsewhere in the room, its colour and composition are in the Etruscan style and more appropriate for the Dressing Room next door than this room.

OTHER FURNITURE

The black and gold japanned commode is comparable to one made by Chippendale for Harewood in 1775. Its carved wood ram's head capitals are gilded to simulate ormolu mounts and correspond to the decoration on Adam's chimney-piece.

The pole fire-screen with a circular panel contains an embroidered design of a monogram SC, Sarah Child. The needlework is much less skilled than the panel done by Mrs Child for the Etruscan Dressing Room screen and may be an early work by her, or her daughter, Sarah Anne. The carved and gilt pole stand is identical to the one that was in the Drawing Room in 1782 and was probably made from the same design, possibly for Berkeley Square or Upton.

The Etruscan Dressing Room

THE ETRUSCAN DRESSING ROOM

Adam's first essay in the Etruscan style of decoration was the dressing-room he created in 1773–4 for the Countess of Derby at Grosvenor Square. He claimed that this was:

unlike anything hitherto practised in Europe, for although the style of the ornament and the colouring . . . are both evidently imitated from the vases and urns of the Etruscans, yet we have not been able to discover, either in our researches into antiquity, or the works of modern artists, any idea of applying this taste to the decoration of apartments.

However, his two alternative designs for the Osterley ceiling, both drawn in 1772, clearly show that the taste was not distinguished by ornament, but rather by black and terracotta colours, which were, as he said, inspired by the Etruscan vases in Sir William Hamilton's collection, published by D'Hancarville in four volumes, starting in 1766.

Adam certainly also knew of the imitation 'antique' tablets and medallions in 'black basaltes with Etruscan red burnt-in grounds' that were being manufactured by Josiah Wedgwood as early as 1769. These tablets were advertised in 1773 as being suitable for 'inlaying . . . in the Pannels of Rooms [and] Chimney Pieces, or for hanging up as ornaments in libraries . . . or as Pictures for Dressing Rooms'. Walpole described the Etruscan Dressing Room in 1778 as being 'painted all over like Wedgwood's ware, with black and yellow small grotesques . . . It is like going out of a palace into a potter's field.'

Piranesi's *Diversi maniere d'adornare i camini* (1769)

Adam's design for the painted ornament in the Etruscan
Dressing Room (Sir John Soane's Museum)

was another precedent and possible model for the general pattern of the wall decoration, with its delicate arches and horizontal bands from which tablets, medallions, cameos and other ornaments are suspended. Adam and Piranesi had met in Rome and admired each other greatly.

Pale sky blue is the ground colour used by Adam for his Etruscan decorations here, at Derby House and at Home House. At Osterley he seems to have been aiming at an open-air effect. Indeed, Walpole saw the Dressing Room as a kind of pergola and thought 'it would be a pretty waiting room in a garden'. But, as a termination to the two 'proud rooms' preceding it, it was inexcusably chilling and 'a profound tumble into the bathos'.

Finished, coloured designs for the wall decorations, showing the chimney-piece, pier-glass and curtain cornices more or less as executed, were made

on 11 October 1775. The vaulted garden room under the perron on the west front was also decorated in the Etruscan style, in 1779.

The survival of the Etruscan Dressing Room unaltered is remarkable, especially after its occasional use as a school-room in the late nineteenth century.

PAINTED ORNAMENT

Pietro Maria Borgnis (?1742–*c*.1810), a figure and ornament painter who had worked with his father, Giuseppe Mattia, and brother Giovanni, at West Wycombe Park and church, painted the ornaments on sheets of paper, which were then pasted on canvas and fixed to the ceiling and walls. The painted canvas chimney-board designed by Adam on 2 June 1777 can also be credited to Borgnis.

FURNITURE

The crest of the pier-glass, designed in May 1775, repeats the painted medallions round the walls, and the seated female figures flanking an openwork basket of flowers correspond to the seated figures over the mantelpiece. Its black and gold border harmonises with the accompanying japanned commode incorporating panels of oriental lacquer and embellished with carved and gilt wood lion's heads. Like the commode in the State Bedchamber, this was probably supplied by Chippendale.

The black and gold japanned pembroke table, painted with a *Scene in the Garden of the Hesperides* after an engraving in Hamilton's *Vases*, was made by Henry Clay of Covent Garden, 'Japanner in Ordinary to His Majesty and His Royal Highness The Prince of Wales'. Its designer is unknown.

Adam's first design for the suite of eight armchairs, dated 25 January 1776, had arms in the shape of griffins and a vase-shaped splat. However, fearsome griffins were evidently considered unsuitable companions for the festive female figures under whom the chairs were to stand, and too masculine for a ladies' dressing-room. The revised design, made on 6 March 1776, is more conventional and painted grey with black and terracotta ornaments to match the walls. The cane seats had grey silk bordered and fringed cushions of the same material as the festoon window curtains. All that remains of the original upholstery are the black and terracotta curtain fringes.

Few Adam rooms were decorated as uniformly as this one. Not only did he design the tripod firescreen painted black and terracotta on a grey ground, but also the needlework panel embroidered by Mrs Child. The panel, designed in November 1776, has a central vase with ram's heads, similar to the chair backs. The pole-screen, designed two years later, has a shaft in the form of a thyrsus and a black-painted tripod stand with lion's feet and masks relating to those on the japanned commode. Sadly, the Etruscan-style workbag, which he designed for Mrs Child to embroider and use, no longer survives.

CARPET

Adam's design for a carpet to answer the ceiling, dated 11 October 1775, is unlikely to have been executed, as no carpet is listed in the 1782 inventory, nor was one noted by Mrs Lybbe Powys when she visited the house in 1788.

THE SOUTH PASSAGE

FURNITURE

On display here is the greater part of a large suite of Chinese black and gold lacquer hall furniture bearing the Child arms. These pieces were almost certainly made in the 1720s for Sir Francis Child the Younger, who was a director of the East India Company in 1718–19 and 1721–35. They were most likely ordered at the same time as the Chinese armorial porcelain (on display in Mr Child's Dressing Room), which was made *c*.1720–5, and, like the porcelain, were destined for Child's London house in Lincoln's Inn Fields. After this house was sold in 1767, the table and eight chairs were sent to Osterley and placed in the vestibule or secondary hall on the ground floor. The other pieces, which are not listed in the 1782 inventory, presumably went to Upton or Berkeley Square or were divided between the two.

Such was the 'profusion of rich China & Japan' at Osterley – porcelain, lacquer furniture, chintzes, India paper, Decca work and so forth – that Agneta Yorke 'could almost fancy [herself] in Pekin'.

THE SOUTH VESTIBULE

CERAMICS

The glazed cabinet, which was bought by the present Lord Jersey in the 1940s, contains more of the Childs' impressive collection of porcelain. Special note should be made of:

Sèvres pear-shaped ewer and cover and shaped oval basin with *bleu-céleste* grounds and panels, painted in colours with amatory trophies enriched with classical quotations of love. This was probably made as a royal marriage gift to the future Louis XVIII or Charles X on their weddings in 1771 and 1773 respectively. The set is listed in the 1860 Berkeley Square inventory.

Sèvres *écuelle* (shallow bowl) with interlaced handles, complete with cover and oval, quatrefoil stand. The stand is painted with a love trophy, and the *écuelle* with panels of cupids said to be after Boucher on a *bleu celeste oeil de perdrix* ground of *pointellé* pattern of small circles bordered by dark blue dots. Their mark dates them 1770. The *écuelle* is listed in the 1860 Berkeley Square inventory.

The view from the portico over the park

CHAPTER SEVEN

THE GARDEN AND PARK

Osterley's 'well wooded' park, 'garnished with manie faire ponds', has always ranked higher than its garden. Indeed, in Glover's survey there is no garden, not even in the fountain court in front of the house where one might be expected. The house is simply set in an enclosure of twenty acres of pasture with an avenue of trees on the west side.

What Rocque found when he came to draw his map in 1741 could not have been more different. The grounds had been laid out in imitation of Hampton Court with a grandiose *patte d'oie* ('goose's foot') of tree-lined avenues radiating from a double semicircle of trees. Nearer the house was a walled kitchen garden and formal wilderness garden on the north side, a T-shaped canal bisected by avenues of trees on the south side, an oval basin on the east front, and a long canal on the west with more avenues stretching from it into that part of the park.

The formal plan suited the flat, open terrain perfectly. It was almost certainly executed for Sir Francis Child the Younger to whom Richard Bradley dedicated the second part of his *Fruit garden display'd* in 1732. The royal gardener Henry Wise (1653–1738) comes to mind as a possible designer, as he and his partner, George London, had supplied the elder Sir Francis with trees for his garden at Parsons Green. However, it seems unlikely that he would have created such a close copy at Osterley of his work for William and Mary at Hampton Court.

The transformation of the formal garden into landscaped pleasure grounds was a gradual process begun in the early 1760s by Francis Child and completed over the next twenty years by his brother, Robert. Ponds and canals were thrown together to form three long, narrow lakes which were juxtaposed in such a way as to give the appearance of a river curving round the house. The pleasure garden was extended and laid out in the latest fashion with lawns and pasture, clumps of trees and shrubbery, and a shaded gravel walk dotted with flowers encompassing the whole. 'Capability' Brown's garden for Lord Holderness next door at Syon Hill may well have been influential, but he himself was not involved at Osterley. Who the designer was is not known.

The Doric Temple was originally part of the formal garden north-west of the house, terminating the avenue west of the wilderness. According to

(Right) Detail of John Rocque's 1741 map of Middlesex showing the tree-lined avenues radiating from the east and west fronts of the pre-Adam house

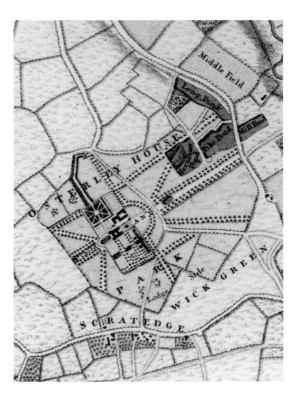

Osterley Park in the mid-eighteenth century; after
Anthony Devis (Gallery)

tradition, it was built in the 1720s by the architect
John James of Greenwich. However, it is not shown
in Rocque's map and is much more likely to have
been built in the late 1740s or early '50s for Samuel
Child. The Rococo plasterwork in the interior was
certainly of that date. This was extensively restored
in the mid-1930s. The medallion heads may sym-
bolise art, literature and the seasons, and their scroll
frames with crossed branches incorporate animal
heads, which represent the Four Elements. After the
avenues were removed, other garden buildings
were introduced to enliven the scene.

A large pedimented Doric orangery, 90 feet long
by 20 feet wide, was built by Adam in 1763–4. It
survived until the Second World War, when a stove
set light to black-out curtains and the building was
burnt down. In Adam's time it was known as the
'great green house' to distinguish it from the smaller
greenhouse, now called the 'Garden House', which

has a semicircular front, stucco medallions of festive
figures and Ionic pilasters. The latter was built in
1780 and is still standing; only the sphinxes at the
ends of its parapet have vanished.

These were the first and last documented garden
buildings by Adam at Osterley. In 1768 he made
alternative designs for a three-arch bridge, 186 feet
long, which was probably intended to be built
across the narrow part of Middle Lake for a drive
from the front of the house directly to Osterley
Lane. It would have been an impressive sight, but
was not executed. Osterley Lane became the main
drive and in 1777 new entrance lodges and gates
designed by Adam were built at the junction with
Wyke Green. This was followed in 1777 by a design
for a rustic, stone bridge with a single arch, which
was built across the narrow end of North (Lower)
Lake connecting the 'old great park' and the

(Right, above) The Doric Temple

(Right, below) The semicircular Garden House

'menagerie park'. It is not clear whether this was part of an unrealised plan to create a shorter route from the house northwards to Windmill Lane and the main London–Oxford road, or simply an ornamental feature in the landscape associated with the menagerie.

Many other garden buildings were erected for Robert Child at Osterley without Adam's intervention. Most of these have vanished without trace, including a painted summer-house with a pair of urns and a bust on its pediment, which were finished in 1764. There was another summer-house furnished in the 1780s with ten green armchairs, an oval dining-table, a square mahogany handkerchief table, two circular marble slabs, two sofas and two aloes in tubs. In 1786 Sophie de la Roche visited a 'Chinese summer-house, where all the furnishings came from China, arranged in the taste and custom of the country'. This was the 'Tea Room in the Garden', which stood near a plantation of winter-flowering viburnum. It had five rooms in all, including two bedrooms and a reception room furnished with a suite of 'India bamboo' armchairs and sofa, and two umbrellas and circular flower stands to take outside.

There was a pine-house in the pinetum near the Orangery, a dog kennel, a deer-house, and a windmill. On the edge of Garden Lake was an ice-house under a mound, and on North Lake a ford, a small brick bridge, and a cascade with iron railings. Apart from these permanent structures there were several temporary ones – a flower stage, a summer-house, an alcove and garden seats – which were brought out for the summer and stored in winter.

The principal attraction was the menagerie, a small wooded and walled 'park within a park' on the east bank of North Lake, reached by a rope-drawn ferry-boat. Agneta Yorke considered it the 'prettiest place [she] ever saw, 'tis an absolute retreat, & fill'd with all sorts of curious and scarce Birds and Fowles, among the rest 2 numidian Cranes that follow like Dogs, and a pair of Chinese teale that have only been seen in England before upon the India paper ...' An expensive secretary bird was a later arrival.

Drawings of the most unusual specimens were made for Robert Child by William Hayes, an ingenious local artist also patronised by the Duchesses of Portland and Northumberland, and hung in the library at Upton where there was a collection of stuffed birds. Hayes, having fallen on hard times, employed some of his 21 children to help him engrave and colour his bird *Portraits*, which he published in two volumes in 1794. Special coloured proofs were made for Sarah Child, then Lady Ducie, to decorate one of the rooms at Menagerie House. This small, pedimented residence flanked by arched bird pens is said to have been designed by Philip Norris, a kinsman of the bricklayer Richard Norris.

Birds were not the only curiosities to be seen at the menagerie. There was a tent in one part, and on the lake a very large sampan and several other colourful pleasure boats.

Keeping a large aviary as well as hot-houses of scarce and valuable plants was exceedingly expensive. Walpole reckoned the cost of the kitchen garden alone was £1,400 a year. Little wonder, therefore, that after the deaths in 1793 of Robert Child's widow and daughter, the trustees sought legal permission to override the terms of his will requiring them to maintain the garden in the same manner as he had done. It was agreed that they should sell the collection of pot plants and cease replenishing the stock of birds, but keep the park and buildings in substantial repair and order. The menagerie evidently remained open to the public on application. In 1802 members of the Academy Club, including Sir John Soane, Joseph Nollekens, Johann Zoffany, Benjamin West and other artists and architects, went there for a summer outing, and had dinner brought in from Ealing. They did not see the house.

Apart from the menagerie, the park was not much admired, being too flat and dull for most tastes. Walpole thought it 'the ugliest spot of ground in the universe'. But that was in 1773, before any serious tree planting. A year later four cedars of Lebanon were purchased in pots for the south side of the house, and in 1780 and 1781 twenty black Antigua pines and approximately 3,000 trees of other sorts were planted with fencing round them. These were supplied by Hugh Ronald, one of the most important nurserymen of the period, whose

View of the Osterley menagerie by Anthony Devis (private collection)

The east front in autumn

garden was conveniently located at Brentford. No doubt the appearance of the park was much altered, but whether it was much improved is another matter. To some the large number of trees, which greatly increased in the nineteenth century, only added to the 'air of seclusion and languor', although the 7th Earl did add rare species to the collection.

During the family's stays at Osterley from 1883, the pleasure grounds were used for garden parties, tennis and boating. On one famous Sunday in 1895 a private secretary to the Tory leader Lord Salisbury arrived hot and dusty, having pedalled to Osterley by bicycle. All he would say was 'Give me an egg beaten up in brandy and find me Arthur Balfour'. When he had regained his breath, he told Balfour, who was playing tennis on the lawn, that the Liberal government had fallen and that they were back in power. With Drake-like coolness, Balfour continued the game as though nothing had happened.

In his short time at Osterley the present Lord Jersey did much to open up vistas by replacing the evergreen Victorian shrubberies with flowers. He rerouted the drive from the Jersey Road Lodge to create from it a direct view of the front of the house and incorporated a large rose garden. He also planted a double herbaceous border between the wall of the kitchen garden and the back of the semicircular Adam Garden House.

The M4, built in 1965, has had a savage effect on the park, but the National Trust has been working to return it to its earlier state. The Great Meadow is now refenced following the evidence of nineteenth-century plans, and the area has been restocked with Limousin cattle. Plans are in progress to reinstate a garden of the 1820s–30s around the Garden House. The pleasure grounds continue in the form of a walk around the grazed area of the Great Meadow which provides access to the garden lake. All these features will be restored to their eighteenth-century form.

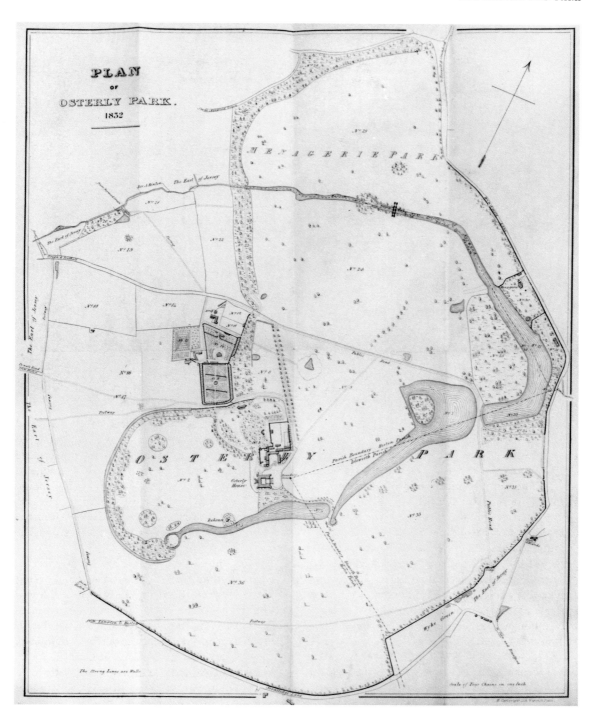

Plan of the park drawn up in 1832, when Osterley was offered for lease (Greater London Record Office)

77

BIBLIOGRAPHY

The Jersey Papers are deposited in the Greater London Record Office and the Victoria & Albert Museum.

ADAM, Robert and James, *The Works in Architecture*, i, ii, 1773–9; iii, 1822.

BOLTON, A.T., *The Architecture of Robert and James Adam*, 2 vols, 1922.

DE LA ROCHE, Sophie, *Sophie in London*, trans. C.Williams, 1933.

FENAILLE, M., *Etat général des tapisseries de la manufacture des Gobelins*, iv, 1907.

FERET, C.J., *Fulham Old and New*, ii, 1900.

GOODISON, Nicholas, *Ormolu: The Work of Matthew Boulton*, 1974.

GRIMAULT, Mr, *A Catalogue of a Collection of Scarce and Valuable Stove, Green-house, and Hardy Plants, . . . at Osterley, . . . which will be sold by auction*, 11 June 1794.

HARDY, John and Maurice TOMLIN, *Osterley Park House*, V & A Museum, 1985.

HARRIS, Eileen, *The Furniture of Robert Adam*, 1962.

HAYES, William, *Portraits of Rare and Curious Birds, . . . from the Menagery of Osterley Park*, 2 vols, 1794, 1799.

HAYWARD, Helena and P. KIRKHAM, *William and John Linnell*, 2 vols, 1980.

HILTON PRICE, F.G., *The Marygold by Temple Bar*, 1902.

JERSEY, George Francis Child-Villiers, 9th Earl of, *Osterley Park*, 1939.

JERSEY, Margaret, Countess of, *Osterley Park and its Memories*, 1920.

JERSEY, Margaret, Countess of, *Fifty-one Years of Victorian Life*, 1923.

JESSOP, Augustus, *The Autobiography of the Hon. Roger North*, 1887.

LYBBE POWYS, Mrs, *Passages from the Diary of Mrs Lybbe Powys*, 1899.

LYSONS, D., *Environs of London*, iii, 1795.

POWELL, Violet, *Margaret Countess of Jersey*, 1971.

ROWAN, Alistair, *Robert Adam, Catalogue of Architectural Drawings in the Victoria and Albert Museum*, 1988.

ROYAL BANK OF SCOTLAND, *Child & Co. The First House in the City*, 1992.

STILLMAN, Damie, *The Decorative Work of Robert Adam*, 1966.

THORNTON, Peter, *Osterley Park*, 1972.

TOMLIN, Maurice, *Catalogue of Adam Period Furniture*, V & A Museum, 1982.

TOMLIN, Maurice, 'Back to Adam at Osterley, Furniture re-arranged to the original designs', *Country Life*, 18 June, 25 June 1970, pp. 1166–8, 1258–60.

TOMLIN, Maurice, 'The 1782 Inventory of Osterley Park', *Furniture History*, xxii, 1986, pp. 107–29.

VICTORIA HISTORY OF THE COUNTIES OF ENGLAND. *A History of the County of Middlesex*, ed. S.Reynolds, iii, 1962.

WALPOLE, Horace, *Correspondence*, Yale ed., xxviii, pp. 413–4, xxxii, pp. 125–7, xxxiv, pp. 237–8.

WARD-JACKSON, Peter, *Osterley Park*, 1953.

YORKE, James, 'Osterley before Adam', *Country Life*, 14 September 1989, pp. 220–2.

INDEX